DEAR TINY SEPUKU

Dear Tiny Sepuku

One Little Cartoon's Bold and Bewildering Love Advice
By Ken Cursoe

**Andrews McMeel
Publishing**

Kansas City

03 04 05 06 07 BBG 10 9 8 7 6 5 4 3 2 1

ISBN: 0-7407-3321-4

Library of Congress Control Number: 2002111008

To my Mom and Dad, friends, family, the loves of my life,
and all the readers who supported Tiny over the years.
None of this would have been possible without you. Thanks.

Love,

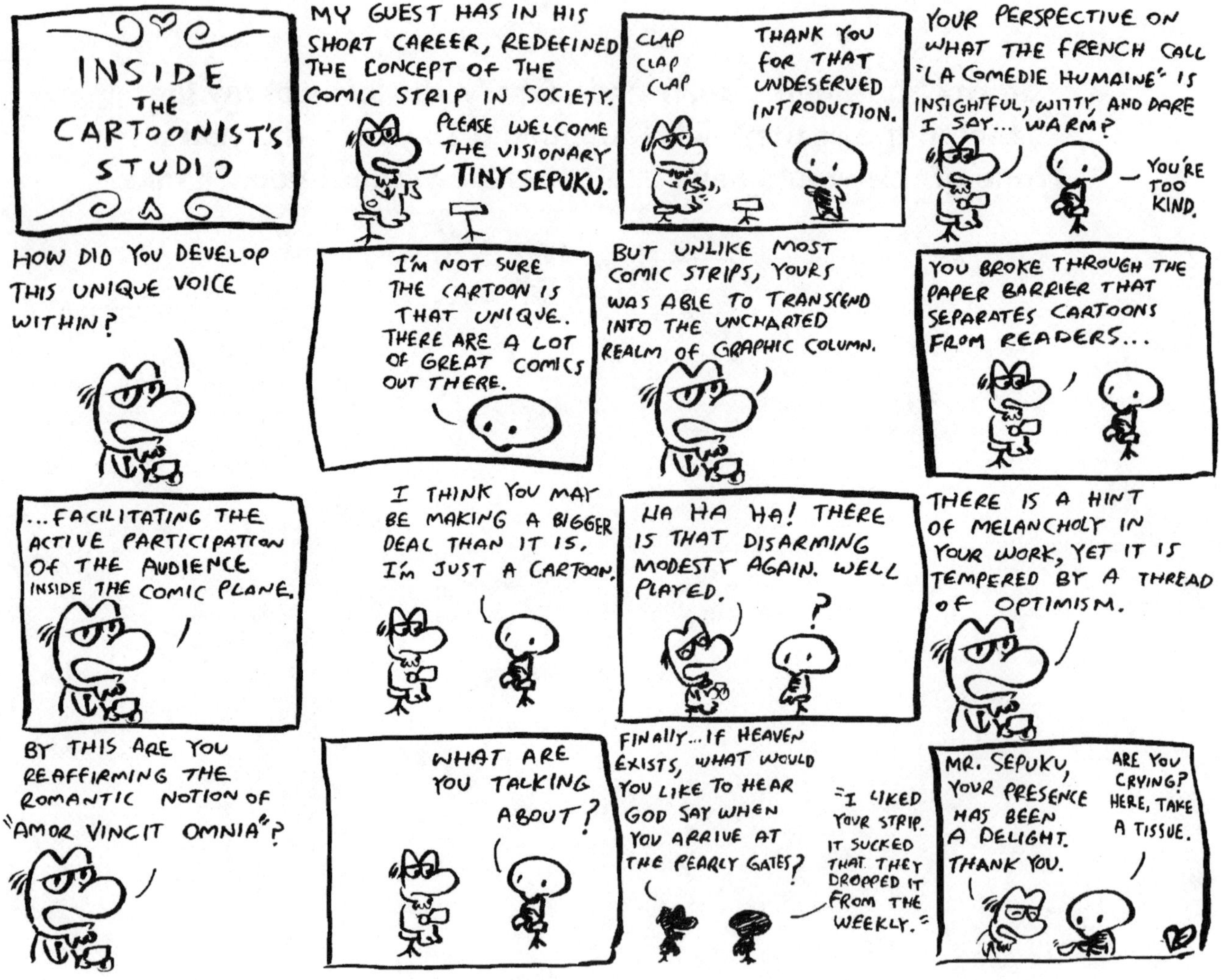
INSIDE THE CARTOONIST'S STUDIO
MY GUEST HAS IN HIS SHORT CAREER, REDEFINED THE CONCEPT OF THE COMIC STRIP IN SOCIETY.
PLEASE WELCOME THE VISIONARY TINY SEPUKU.
CLAP CLAP CLAP
THANK YOU FOR THAT UNDESERVED INTRODUCTION.
YOUR PERSPECTIVE ON WHAT THE FRENCH CALL "LA COMEDIE HUMAINE" IS INSIGHTFUL, WITTY, AND DARE I SAY... WARM?
YOU'RE TOO KIND.
HOW DID YOU DEVELOP THIS UNIQUE VOICE WITHIN?
I'M NOT SURE THE CARTOON IS THAT UNIQUE. THERE ARE A LOT OF GREAT COMICS OUT THERE.
BUT UNLIKE MOST COMIC STRIPS, YOURS WAS ABLE TO TRANSCEND INTO THE UNCHARTED REALM OF GRAPHIC COLUMN.
YOU BROKE THROUGH THE PAPER BARRIER THAT SEPARATES CARTOONS FROM READERS...
...FACILITATING THE ACTIVE PARTICIPATION OF THE AUDIENCE INSIDE THE COMIC PLANE.
I THINK YOU MAY BE MAKING A BIGGER DEAL THAN IT IS. I'M JUST A CARTOON.
HA HA HA! THERE IS THAT DISARMING MODESTY AGAIN. WELL PLAYED.
?
THERE IS A HINT OF MELANCHOLY IN YOUR WORK, YET IT IS TEMPERED BY A THREAD OF OPTIMISM.
BY THIS ARE YOU REAFFIRMING THE ROMANTIC NOTION OF "AMOR VINCIT OMNIA"?
WHAT ARE YOU TALKING ABOUT?
FINALLY... IF HEAVEN EXISTS, WHAT WOULD YOU LIKE TO HEAR GOD SAY WHEN YOU ARRIVE AT THE PEARLY GATES?
"I LIKED YOUR STRIP. IT SUCKED THAT THEY DROPPED IT FROM THE WEEKLY."
MR. SEPUKU, YOUR PRESENCE HAS BEEN A DELIGHT. THANK YOU.
ARE YOU CRYING? HERE, TAKE A TISSUE.

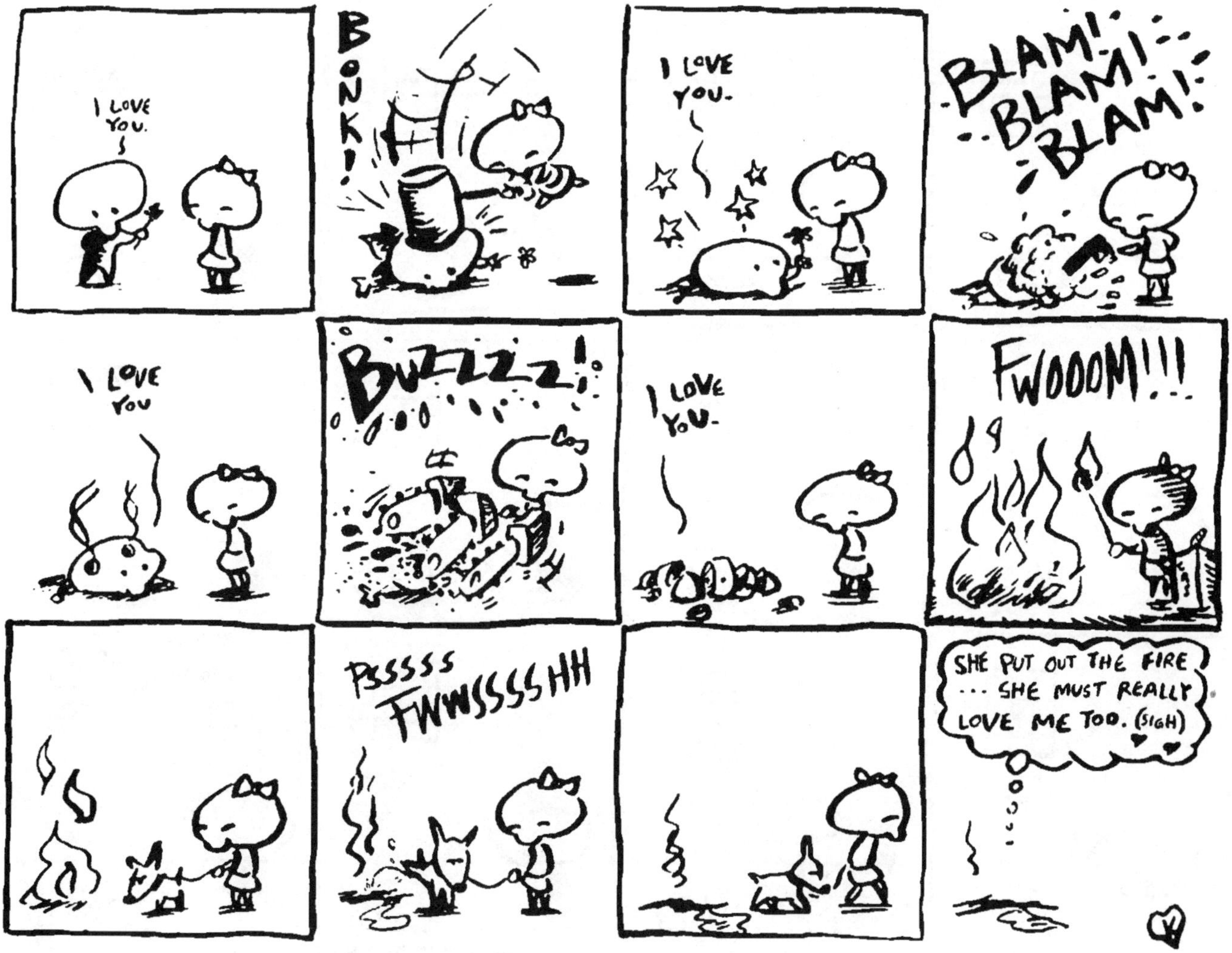
I LOVE YOU.
BONK!
I LOVE YOU.
BLAM! BLAM! BLAM!
I LOVE YOU
BUZZZZ!
I LOVE YOU.
FWOOOM!!!
PSSSSS
FWSSSSSHH
SHE PUT OUT THE FIRE ... SHE MUST REALLY LOVE ME TOO. (SIGH)

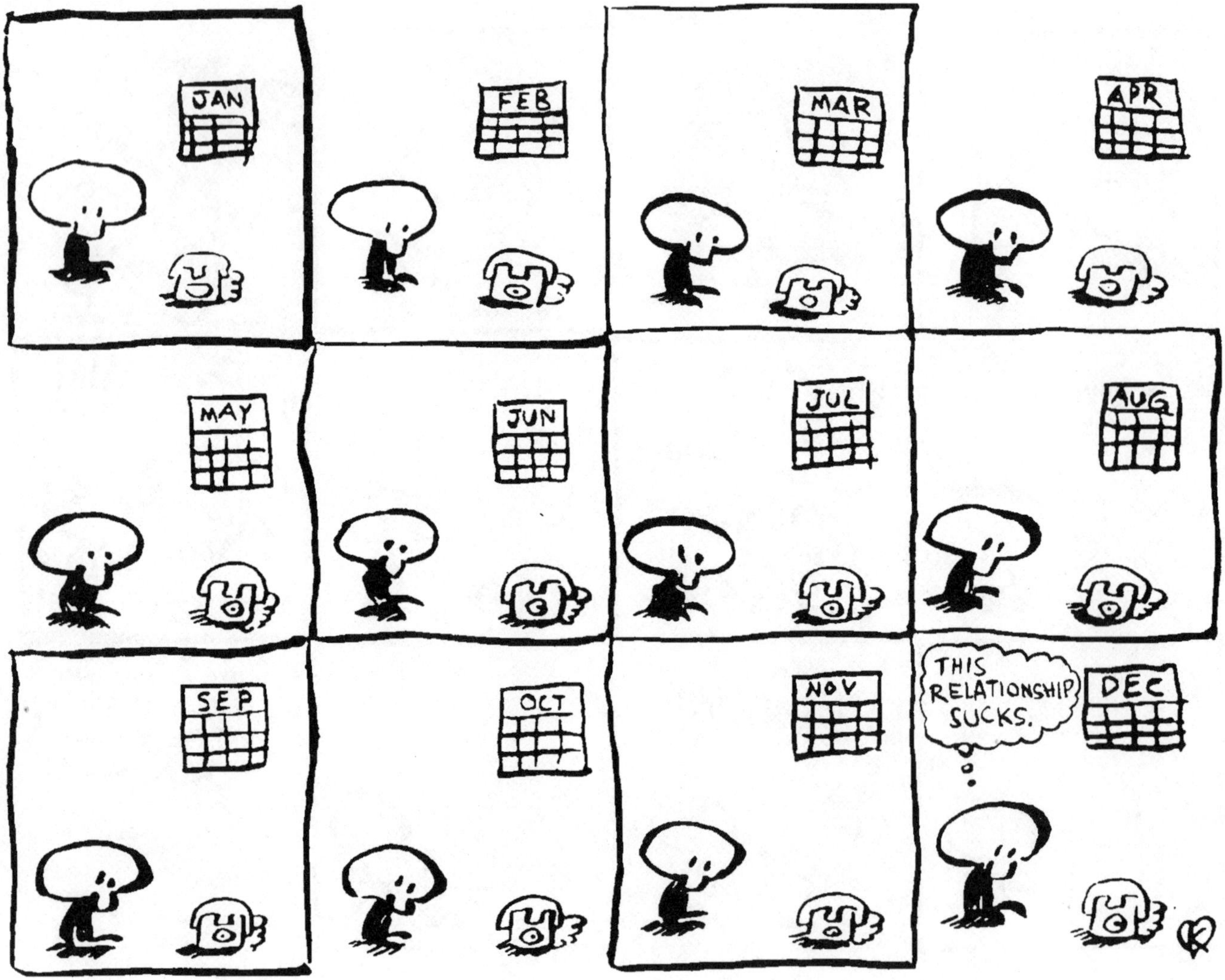
JAN
FEB
MAR
APR
MAY
JUN
JUL
AUG
SEP
OCT
NOV
THIS RELATIONSHIP SUCKS.
DEC

WHEN SILVER LEFT TO PERSUE OTHER MEN...

I FILLED MYSELF WITH POISONED BLADES.

WHEN EMMA WISHED TO BE SINGLE AGAIN...

I KILLED MYSELF WITH HAND GRENADES.

WHEN RAIN GREW TIRED OF MY HEART...

I HUNG MYSELF FROM A WILLOW TREE.

WHEN ELISA REFUSED MY LOVE TO START...

I DROWNED MYSELF IN THE COLD, DARK SEA.

WHEN JANE MARRIED ANOTHER GUY...

I SHOT MYSELF IN DESPAIR.

AND NOW I MUST DEVISE A NEW WAY TO DIE...

'CUZ I JUST MET A GIRL NAMED CLAIRE.

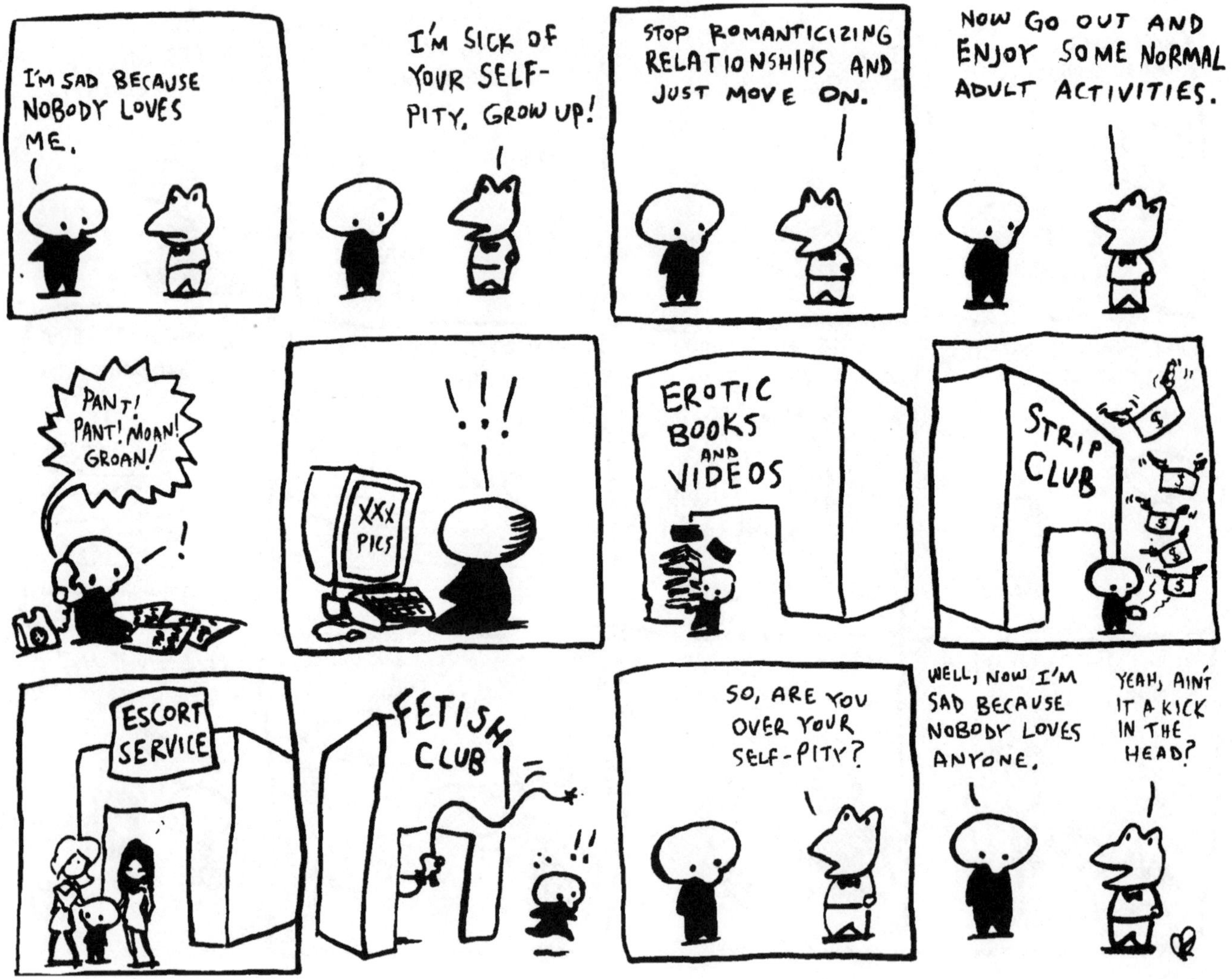
I'M SAD BECAUSE NOBODY LOVES ME.
I'M SICK OF YOUR SELF-PITY. GROW UP!
STOP ROMANTICIZING RELATIONSHIPS AND JUST MOVE ON.
NOW GO OUT AND ENJOY SOME NORMAL ADULT ACTIVITIES.
PANT! PANT! MOAN! GROAN!
!
!!!
XXX PICS
EROTIC BOOKS AND VIDEOS
STRIP CLUB
ESCORT SERVICE
FETISH CLUB
!!
SO, ARE YOU OVER YOUR SELF-PITY?
WELL, NOW I'M SAD BECAUSE NOBODY LOVES ANYONE.
YEAH, AIN'T IT A KICK IN THE HEAD?

SHE SAYS IT'S NOT 'CAUSE HE'S RICHER...

OR MORE SUCCESSFUL, OR MORE EDUCATED.

SHE SAYS IT'S NOT 'CAUSE HE'S STRONGER...

OR BETTER LOOKING, OR SOPHISTICATED.

SHE SAYS IT'S NOT 'CAUSE HE'S FUNNER TO BE WITH...

OR THAT SHE FEELS MORE AT EASE WITH HIM OVER ME.

SHE SAYS IT'S NOT 'CAUSE HE'S MORE ROMANTIC...

AND HIS PASSION FOR HER SETS HER FREE.

SHE SAYS IT'S NONE OF THOSE THINGS THAT MADE HER GO...

AND I SHOULDN'T FEEL SAD OR BLUE.

BUT ALL SHE SAYS TO ME ARE LIES...

AND THEY STARTED WHEN SHE SAID "I LOVE YOU."

WE'VE BEEN TOGETHER A WHILE, AND I THINK YOU SHOULD KNOW...

I LOVE YOU.

!!!

OH...UH... COULD YOU WAIT HERE? I'LL BE RIGHT BACK.

?

SMOOCH SMOOCH KISS SMACK SLOBBER

THANK YOU MA'AM! MAY I HAVE ANOTHER!

BZZZZ

HMMM

OK... I LOVE YOU TOO!

REALLY? WAIT HERE A SEC...

Dear T.S.,

How long should I wait to call someone after the first date?
— Rene
Havre, MT

Tiny Sepuku & Sepukutie in "The Calling Game"

THE DAY AFTER...

A COUPLE DAYS LATER...

A FEW MORE DAYS...

SEVERAL DAYS...

WEEKS...

I GUESS SHE'S NOT INTERESTED.

JERK.

13

"BETTY" FROM TEXAS WRITES:

"I AM A SINGLE MOTHER WITH THREE CHILDREN AND HAVE BEEN DIVORCED FOR 5 YEARS NOW. 2 OF MY CHILDREN ARE NOW IN HIGH SCHOOL, THE 3RD IS IN COLLEGE."

"I HAVEN'T DATED ANYONE DURING THIS TIME AS TO NOT UPSET MY CHILDREN. I'VE TRIED TO TALK TO THEM ABOUT IT RECENTLY AND THEY STILL DON'T SEEM TO LIKE THE IDEA..."

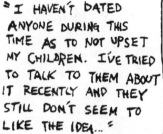

"...BUT I AM LONGING FOR MALE COMPANIONSHIP. WHAT SHOULD I DO?"

WELL, "BETTY," THAT'S A TOUGH QUESTION.

MY ADVICE TO YOU IS TO PRETEND TO HAVE A BOYFRIEND.

SEND YOURSELF LOVE LETTERS AND FLOWERS...

MORE FLOWERS FOR MOI? TEE HEE.

PLAY LIKE YOU'RE ON THE PHONE WITH HIM...

I WUV YOU TOO SNUGGLE BUTT.

GO ON MAKE BELIEVE DATES AND TRIPS.

DON'T WAIT UP, KIDS, I'M HAVING DINNER IN PARIS TONIGHT.

EVENTUALLY YOUR KIDS WILL FIND OUT IT'S ALL A SHAM.

I THINK MOM'S FLIPPED.   I'M SCARED.

WHEN THEY DO, THEY'LL STRONGLY ENCOURAGE YOU TO DATE OTHER MEN.

I KNOW THIS PSYCHIATRIST YOU SHOULD MEET.   YEAH, HE'S REALLY NICE.   OH?

I HOPE THAT HELPS. GOOD LUCK "BETTY." TAKE CARE EVERYONE.

NASTY NARI FROM SAN FRANCISCO ASKS, "WHY DON'T MEN EXPRESS THEIR INNER FEELINGS?"

WELL I HAD A LOT OF ANSWERS FOR THIS... BUT I DECIDED TO ASK AN AVERAGE GUY WHY HE DOESN'T SHOW HIS INNER FEELINGS.

SO CARE TO ANSWER THE QUESTION?

WELL FIRST OFF CHICKS DON'T WANT GUYS TO EXPRESS THEIR FEELINGS.

THEY DON'T?

NO WAY, MAN. THEY RESPECT EMOTIONALLY EXPRESSIVE GUYS LIKE MEN RESPECT PROMISCUOUS WOMEN. YOU DATE 'EM BUT IT'S NOT SERIOUS.

YA SEE, CHICKS WANT A GUY WHO'S ALL CLOSED UP AND THOUGHTLESS SO THEY CAN BE THE FIRST TO GET BEYOND THAT TOUGH EXTERIOR.

I SHOW 'EM A LITTLE BIT OF ATTENTION, TAKE 'EM OUT ONCE IN A WHILE, AND DROP AN "I ♡ U" OCCASIONALLY...

... AND SHE THINKS THAT ALL HER HARD WORK AND EFFORT HAS PAID OFF 'CUZ SHE'S "GETTING THROUGH TO ME."

AND GET THIS, SHE'S ALL FULL OF PRIDE 'CUZ SHE CAN TELL HER FRIENDS AND FAMILY "YOU DON'T KNOW HIM LIKE I DO" OR "YOU DON'T SEE HIS SWEETER SIDE."

SHE CONVINCES HERSELF THAT SHE HAS SOME EXCLUSIVE BOND WITH ME THAT NO ONE ELSE CAN UNDERSTAND. HA!

AND IT'S COOL 'CUZ IF SHE CATCHES ME FOOLIN' AROUND, I JUST SAY "IT DIDN'T MEAN ANYTHING, IT'S JUST PHYSICAL" AND SHE BUYS IT!

SO YOU DON'T EXPRESS YOUR FEELINGS SO YOU CAN PLAY SICK MIND GAMES?

WHAT FEELINGS?

YOU'RE A DISGUSTING EXCUSE FOR A MAN... I THINK YOU'D BETTER GET OUT OF MY SIGHT.

YEAH, WELL AT LEAST I'M NOT GOIN' HOME ALONE, LOSER.

DEAR TINY SEPUKU,
IT'S BEEN 4 YEARS SINCE I FINISHED COLLEGE AND I'M STILL HAVING TROUBLE FINDING A DECENT JOB. WHAT CAN I DO? -AL SEATTLE WA

WELL IT SOUNDS LIKE YOU HAVE THE SAME PROBLEM A LOT OF US FACE IN THE SO-CALLED "REAL WORLD".

BUT FEAR NOT, YOU NEED ONLY FOLLOW THESE FOUR SIMPLE STEPS TO LAND A SUCCESSFUL CAREER.

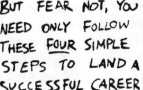

#1. EMBELLISH YOUR RÉSUMÉ:
"INSTEAD OF SAYING YOU WORK AS A CASHIER OR IN FAST FOODS..."

"...SAY YOU ARE A CONSUMER AGENT OR A NUTRITION COUNSELOR".

#2. GET NOTICED:
"YOUR RÉSUMÉ HAS TO STAND OUT AMONG MORE QUALIFIED APPLICANTS. TRY INCLUDING A CENTERFOLD..."

WOW!

"...OR CLEVER PACKAGING..."

DON'T BE A "FOOL"! HIRE THE BEST! ♪♫

"...OR THE PERSONAL TOUCH."

IF YOU EVER WANT TO SEE YOUR BELOVED PET AGAIN YOU WILL HIRE ME.

#3. FOLLOWING UP:
IT'S VERY IMPORTANT TO CALL AFTERWARDS. IT SHOWS PERSISTANCE, DEDICATION, AND EAGERNESS.

MY GOD! IT'S 3:00 AM! HOW'D YOU FIND THIS NUMBER?! I JUST HAD IT CHANGED!!!

#4. THE INTERVIEW:
THIS DETERMINES YOUR PROFESSIONAL FATE. YOU CAN SUCCEED IF YOU GO PREPARED.

WHAT'S THE BASEBALL BAT FOR?

THAT DEPENDS ON HOW YOU ANSWER THIS QUESTION: "DO I GET THE JOB?"

DEAR TINY,
I LIKE A LADY WHO DATES VERY SUCCESSFUL MEN, AM I KIDDING MYSELF BY PURSUING HER?
— AL BELLEVUE WA

SUCCESS DOES NOT EQUATE TO LOVE. LET'S SEE WHAT YOU TWO CAN OFFER IN A RELATIONSHIP.

YOU: NICE, UNDERACHIEVING, POOR, HESITANT, NAIVE, PREDICTABLE, UNSURE, ACCOMMODATING, A DEFERRER, AVERAGE LOOKING, STORY BOOK ROMANTIC

HIM: ROGUISH, AMBITIOUS, RICH, DECISIVE, WORLDLY, IMPULSIVE, CONFIDENT, INFLUENTIAL, AN INITIATOR, VERY ATTRACTIVE, ROMANCE NOVEL ROMANTIC

YOU SAY:
I LOVE YOU.

FLOWER

HE SAYS:
I WANT YOU.

DIAMOND

YOUR DATE:
I MADE YOUR FAVORITE MEAL.

HIS DATE:
I MADE RESERVATIONS AT YOUR FAVORITE RESTAURANT... IN **PARIS.**

YOUR GIFTS:
I KNOW HOW MUCH YOU LIKE ANTIQUES, SO I BOUGHT THIS FOR YOU.

HIS GIFTS:
I KNOW HOW MUCH YOU LIKE ANTIQUES, SO I BOUGHT A SHOP FOR YOU.

DEED

I THINK THE CHOICE IS OBVIOUS:

I WROTE A SONG FOR YOU.

I PRODUCED A MUSIC VIDEO FOR YOU.

...SAY... FORGET HER, DO YOU WANNA GO OUT WITH ME?

17

DEAR TINY,
   I'M MEETING AN OLD LOVER I HAVEN'T SEEN IN YEARS. I'M REALLY NERVOUS ABOUT IT. HELP! —ANGEL SEATTLE, WA

DRAMATIZATION:

WOW! IT'S BEEN YEARS! MY GOD YOU LOOK BEAUTIFUL. WHAT HAVE YOU DONE WITH YOUR LIFE?

WELL... AFTER WE BROKE UP I FINISHED MY DOUBLE MAJOR...

=...THEN I MODELED IN EUROPE TO GET SOME MONEY FOR GRAD SCHOOL=
BELLA BELLA
CLICK CLICK

=...I MET AND LIVED WITH A COMPOSER IN LONDON...=
I WROTE ANOTHER OPERA FOR YOU.
HOW SWEET.

=...I CAME BACK TO THE U.S. TO RECEIVE A FELLOWSHIP AT HARVARD=
THE BOARD AND I GOT YOU A BMW TOO.

=...BUT BEFORE THAT I LIVED AND WORKED WITH A SOFTWARE MOGUL IN NYC=
I WROTE A NEW OPERATING SYSTEM FOR YOU.
HOW SWEET.

=...I FINISHED MY PH.D. AND DECIDED TO HELP CHILDREN IN WAR-TORN COUNTRIES.=

... NOW I'M BACK TO RAISE MONEY FOR THEM WITH MY 3-PICTURE DEAL I'M WRITING FOR DREAMWORKS.

BUT YOU DON'T WANT TO HEAR ABOUT ME, WHAT HAVE YOU BEEN DOING ALL THESE YEARS?

THINKING ABOUT YOU. WONDERING IF YOU EVER THOUGHT ABOUT ME.

YOU STILL KNOW HOW TO MAKE ME LAUGH.

DEAR TINY,

HOW COME WOMEN FALL OUT OF LOVE WITH ME SO FAST? ARE THEY SO BLIND THAT THEY DON'T SEE WHO I REALLY AM? OR AM I SO SUBCONSCIOUSLY FAKE IT TAKES THEM A WHILE TO SEE THROUGH ME? — LLYWELYN, BALLARD, WA

I'VE LEARNED A LOT ABOUT WHY MY RELATIONSHIPS TURNED SOUR BY ASKING MY FORMER LOVERS WHAT WENT WRONG. LET ME SHARE THEIR INSIGHT.

I DON'T OWE YOU AN EXPLANATION.

ALL I CAN SAY IS IT'S NOT YOU, IT'S ME.

LET'S NOT DWELL ON IT, LET'S FORGET ABOUT IT AND MOVE ON.

"THINGS" CHANGE.

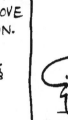

IF YOU DON'T KNOW, WHY SHOULD I TELL YOU?

YOU WOULDN'T UNDERSTAND IF I TOLD YOU.

WHY ARE YOU ASKING ME?

19

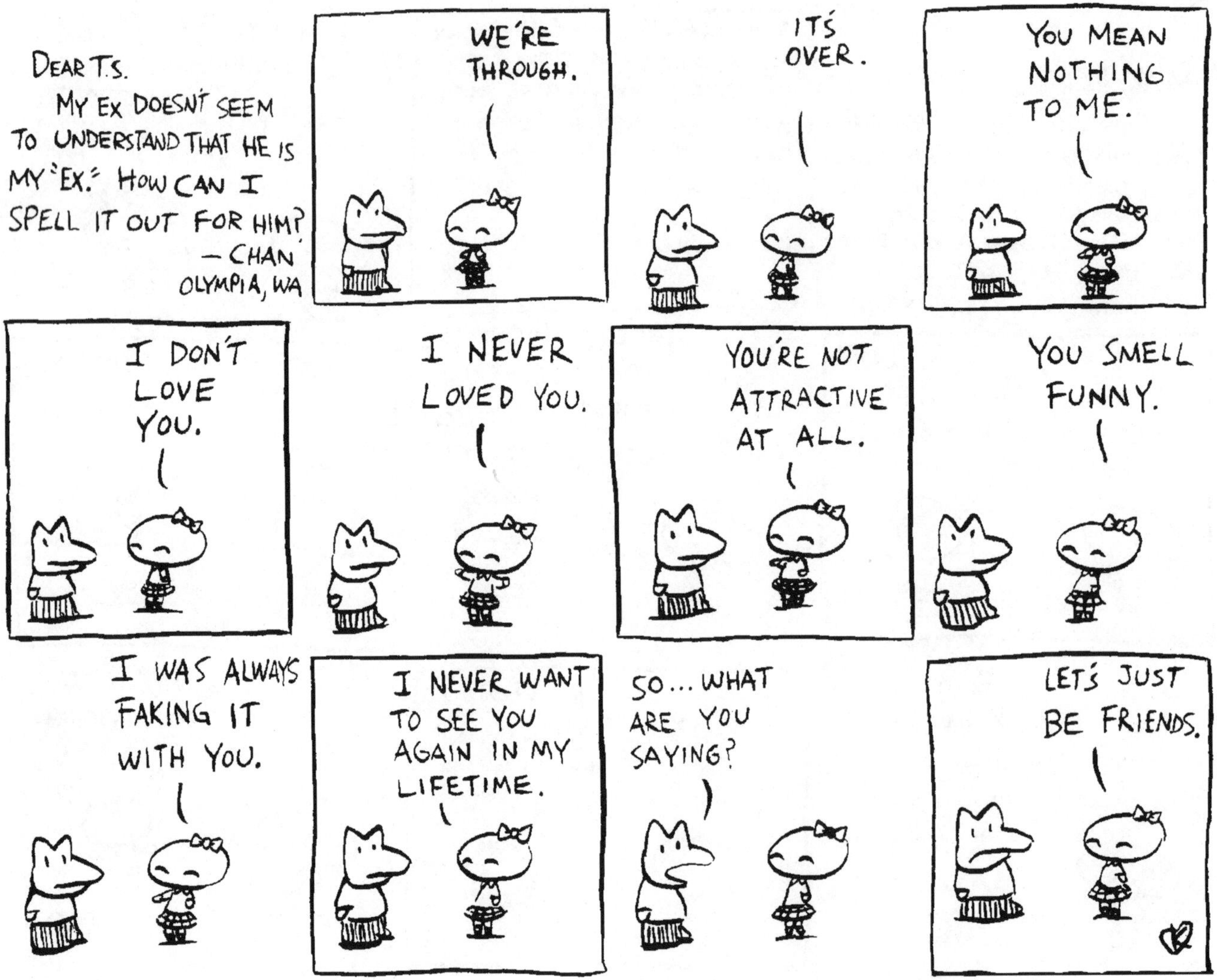
DEAR T.S.
MY EX DOESN'T SEEM TO UNDERSTAND THAT HE IS MY "EX." HOW CAN I SPELL IT OUT FOR HIM?
— CHAN
OLYMPIA, WA
WE'RE THROUGH.
IT'S OVER.
YOU MEAN NOTHING TO ME.
I DON'T LOVE YOU.
I NEVER LOVED YOU.
YOU'RE NOT ATTRACTIVE AT ALL.
YOU SMELL FUNNY.
I WAS ALWAYS FAKING IT WITH YOU.
I NEVER WANT TO SEE YOU AGAIN IN MY LIFETIME.
SO... WHAT ARE YOU SAYING?
LET'S JUST BE FRIENDS.

Dear Tiny,
    Should I persue the girl of my dreams even though she rejects me?
            — Stewart
            Seattle, WA

 To attract the girl of your dreams,

 You must become the boy of her dreams.

 You're nice but not what I want.

 UNIVER$ITY

 WOODRING GYM

 DR. BILL ORTHODONTIST

 ARMANI — FINANCING AVAILABLE

 STATUS DEALER

 BIGSHOT COMPANY

 Wow! You're everything I ever wanted.

 Why can't I ever meet guys like you?

21

DEAR TINY,
DOES "PRINCE CHARMING"
EXIST OR AM I CLINGING
TO AN OLD-FASHIONED
FANTASY? — KIKA
SANTA MONICA, CA

WHAT'S YOUR SECRET?
WHY DO ALL THE
LADIES LOVE YOU
SO MUCH?

ARE YOU SERIOUS? I'M
HANDSOME, RICH, FAMOUS,
POWERFUL, I'M GOOD
WITH A SWORD,
AND I COME
FROM A VERY
PRESTIGIOUS
BACKGROUND.

I ALSO OWN A PALACE,
SERVANTS, VILLAGES,
AND HOLD THE MOST
EXTRAVAGANT BALLS
IN ALL THE
LAND.

WOW, I CAN SEE
WHY EVERYONE
WANTS TO LIVE
HAPPILY EVER
AFTER WITH
YOU.

HA! THEY
WISH!

THEY'RE COMMONERS!
I'M ROYALTY!

WE CAN NEVER
HAVE ANYTHING
SERIOUS BETWEEN
US.

IT'S PRIVILEGE
ENOUGH FOR THEM
TO BE PLEASURED
BY ME.

AT LEAST I CAN PROVIDE
THEM A CHERISHED MEMORY
IN THEIR MUNDANE,
UNSOPHISTICATED
EXISTENCE.

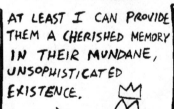

YOU'RE NOT
VERY NOBLE
FOR A PRINCE.

DON'T GUYS
LIKE YOU
GET TURNED
INTO FROGS?

DOESN'T STOP
THE LADIES
FROM KISSIN'
ME, PEASANT.

DEAR TINY,

DOES IT EVER WORK OUT WHEN A STUDENT GETS A CRUSH ON A TEACHER?
— CRUSHER
SEATTLE, WA

I KNOW IT'S A TYPICAL FANTASY, BUT DO YOU REALLY WANT TO BE MORE THAN A TEACHER'S PET?

"SURE THE HOMEWORK WOULD BE GREAT..."

HE ALWAYS STUDIES SO HARD IN HIS ROOM. I'M SO PROUD.

THAT'S MY BOY.

...BUT LOOK AT THE DOWNSIDE.

"SCHOOL WON'T END WHEN THE BELL RINGS."

I WANT YOU TO STAY AFTER CLASS AND TAKE A MAKE-UP EXAM.

V.D. TEST

"YOU'LL BE GRADED ON EVERYTHING."

I'LL GIVE YOU CREDIT FOR EFFORT, BUT I'M ONLY GIVING YOU A "C+" FOR PERFORMANCE.

"YOU CAN'T BE ABSENT OR TARDY."

SORRY I'M LATE.

DO YOU HAVE A NOTE?

"CONVERSATIONS WILL BE A CHALLENGE."

MS. TEACHER, I WANTED TO ASK Y...

UH-UH. DID WE RAISE OUR HAND TO BE CALLED ON?

"AND WHAT IF THEY GET SICK?"

HELLO. I'M MR. JONES. I'LL BE YOUR SUBSTITUTE TODAY.

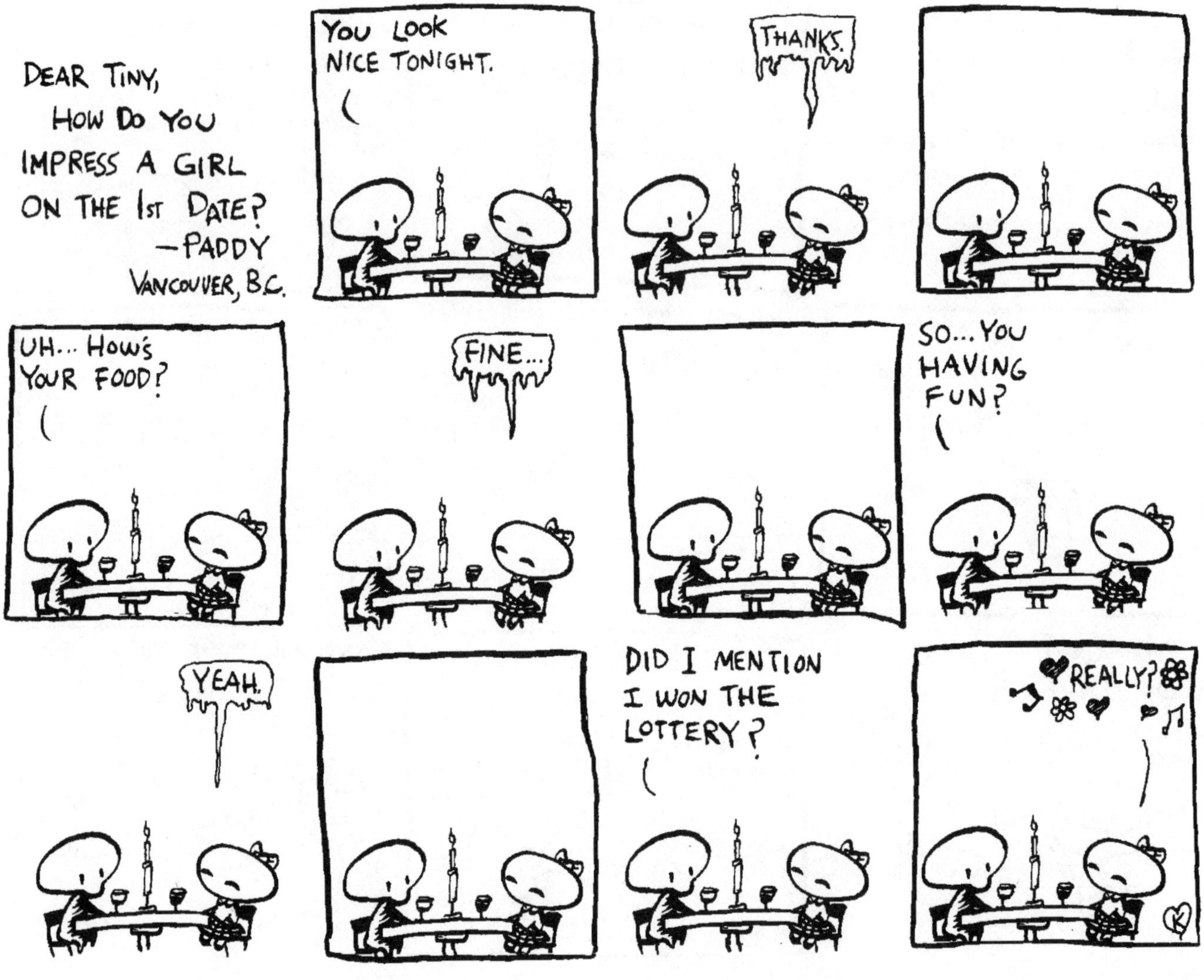
DEAR TINY,
HOW DO YOU IMPRESS A GIRL ON THE 1ST DATE?
—PADDY
VANCOUVER, B.C.
YOU LOOK NICE TONIGHT.
THANKS.
UH... HOW'S YOUR FOOD?
FINE...
SO... YOU HAVING FUN?
YEAH.
DID I MENTION I WON THE LOTTERY?
REALLY?

I NEED IDEAS
FOR *THINGS*
I CAN EAT
OFF MY PARTNER!
— FROSTY
BALLARD, WA

ALPHABET SOUP

I'LL GET A SPOON.

MAYONNAISE

OH BOY! WHERE'S THAT SPOON?

E-Z CHEEZ
(CHEESE IN A CAN)

ARE YOU AS TURNED ON AS I AM?

PASTE

MMMF! MMMF! MMMF!

WHY WON'T YOU OPEN YOUR MOUTH?

20 oz T-BONE

HURRY!! THE GREASE IS HOT!!

CHEWING TOBACCO

PTOOO!

YOU NEVER SWALLOW.

TOOTHPASTE

ARE YOU SURE YOU CAN EAT THIS STUFF? WHAT'S THIS WARNING ON THE TUBE?

VITAMINS

LOOK HOW CUTE, A DINOSAUR.

KIMCHI

MUNCH MUNCH MUNCH

FISH FOOD

...NOW GET DRESSED LIKE A MERMAID!

BENIHANA STYLE STIR-FRY DINNER

THEY MAKE IT LOOK SO EASY AT THE RESTAURANT.

DEAR TINY,
WHAT ARE SOME GOOD SONGS TO PUT YOU IN THE MOOD FOR SWEET LOVIN'?
— MARK
S.L.C., UT

=MY DING-A-LING! MY DING-A-LING!=

JOHN TESH'S "SAX ON THE BEACH" ALBUM. MAKE OUT CITY DUDE!

= HIGH ON A HILL IS A LONELY GOAT HERD LAY-DEE-YO-DOL-LAY -DEE-YO-DOL-LAY...

ANY POP SONG THAT HAS 5 GUYS WAILING FIVE DIFFERENT TUNES AT THE SAME TIME. NOW THAT'S HOT!

="WE ARE SI-A-ME-EEZ IF YOU PLE-EEZ"

IT'S EITHER JIM NEIGHBORS OR BARRY WHITE. I GET THEM CONFUSED.

= 99 BOTTLES OF BEER ON THE WALL, 99 BOTTLES OF BEER...=

OH MAN, ANYTHING BY WEIRD AL YANKOVIC! HE DRIVES THE LADIES WILD!

="I CAN BRING HOME THE BACON, FRY IT UP IN A PAN, AND NEVER EVER MAKE YOU FORGET YOU'RE A MAN, 'CUZ I'M A WOMAN."

THE THEME TO =BATTLESTAR GALACTICA.= A MUST DURING FOREPLAY.

="MY BALONEY HAS A FIRST NAME IT'S O-S-C-A-R..."=

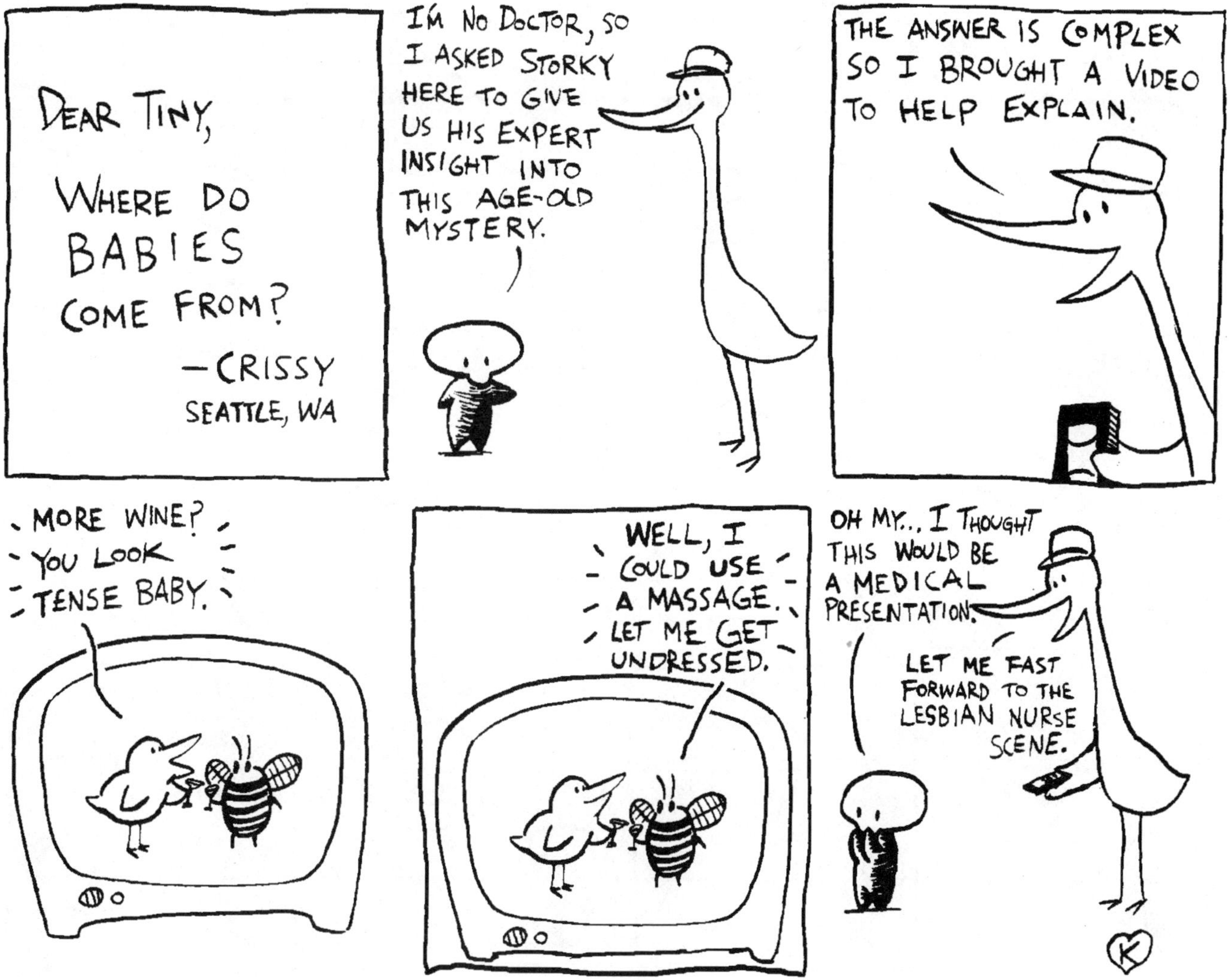

DEAR TINY,
WHERE DO BABIES COME FROM?
—CRISSY
SEATTLE, WA
I'M NO DOCTOR, SO I ASKED STORKY HERE TO GIVE US HIS EXPERT INSIGHT INTO THIS AGE-OLD MYSTERY.
THE ANSWER IS COMPLEX SO I BROUGHT A VIDEO TO HELP EXPLAIN.
MORE WINE? YOU LOOK TENSE BABY.
WELL, I COULD USE A MASSAGE. LET ME GET UNDRESSED.
OH MY... I THOUGHT THIS WOULD BE A MEDICAL PRESENTATION.
LET ME FAST FORWARD TO THE LESBIAN NURSE SCENE.
K

Dear Tiny,
How do you
let go of
an old love?
—"N"
San Francisco, CA

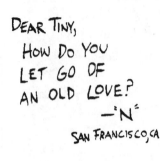

10 YEARS AGO...

9 YEARS AGO...

8 YEARS AGO...

7 YEARS AGO...

6 YEARS AGO...

5 YEARS AGO...

4 YEARS AGO...

3 YEARS AGO...

2 YEARS AGO...

1 YEAR AGO...

TODAY...

Dear Tiny,

Whenever I hang out with my former boyfriend, things get really awkward. What can I do about these uncomfortable moments?
— Mari, Seattle, WA

Try one of these tips to cure a pregnant pause.

1. "Burst out in free-form verse."

Our silence deafens us with memories and regret.

2. "Start miming."

What's wrong? Are you okay? Should I go?

3. "Bring a puppet."

Mr. Dinkle, I'd like you to meet my ex.

"So you're the guy who needs viagra."

4. "Mimic them."

Stop it. I'm serious. Quit it! Ahhhigh!!!

Stop it. I'm serious. Quit it! Ahhhigh!!!

5. "Scat!"

Adooba adooba ah-dooba ba-wa ba-wa bap-ba badabop!!

Well look at the time...

6. "Save them."

Have you heard the good news?

Uh-oh

7. "Talk about work."

So is it weird that I'm your boss now?

8. "Start trouble."

Hey! Tough guy! My friend doesn't like your attitude

9. "Talk about your current relationship."

... I never want to leave the bed when I'm with him.

10. "Break out your fantasy card game."

Hey... where are you going? I wanna show you my magic monkey.

29

DEAR TINY,
DOES TRUE LOVE ALWAYS GO UNREQUITED?
—LOST
SEATTLE, WA.

"THANKS FOR WAITING."

Dear Tiny,

I'm crazy about a guy who seems attracted to me too, but I'm afraid to let him know how I feel. How can I tell for sure if the feelings are mutual?
— MARY ANN
SEATTLE, WA

Dear Tiny,

She's in Vancouver (B.C.), I'm in Seattle. Will Customs crack down on a captivating cross border affair? — Joe, Seattle, WA

P.S. we are BOTH Canadian

I REALLY DON'T KNOW MUCH ABOUT CUSTOMS OR IMMIGRATION LAWS...

...SO I CONSULTED THIS BORDER PATROL AGENT.

SHOULD THIS GUY BE WORRIED?   YES!

WHAT HE IS DOING IS A FELONY WORTHY OF THE DEATH PENALTY!

AMERICANS PAY TRILLIONS OF DOLLARS TO KEEP OUR BORDER WITH CANADA SECURE...

...THEN NAFTA OPENS THE DOOR TO ALL SORTS OF DEVIANTS!

TENS OF MILLIONS OF CANADIANS SNEAK INTO THE U.S. EVERY MINUTE AND STEAL OUR CARS AND PETS!

MANY OF THEM ARE SATANIC COMMUNISTS HIGH ON REEFER!

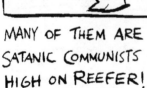

YOU CAN SEE THE URGENT NEED TO DISCOURAGE CROSS BORDER RELATIONSHIPS.

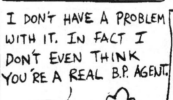

I DON'T HAVE A PROBLEM WITH IT. IN FACT I DON'T EVEN THINK YOU'RE A REAL B.P. AGENT.

SAVE IT FOR THE DEPORTATION HEARING, HIPPY! WHAT KIND OF NAME IS "SEPUKU" ANYWAY?

DEAR T.S.,
  I'VE HEARD EATING CHOCOLATE TRIGGERS THE SAME FEELING OF "LOVE." IS THAT TRUE? — SANDY SEATTLE, WA

I HEARD THAT TOO. HERE ARE SOME OTHER FOODS AND THEIR SIDE EFFECTS.

MEAT — GUILT

MURDERER!

TOFU — ALIENATION

WEIRDO HIPPY FREAK!

FUSION FOOD — HIP

MORE BURRITO VINDALOO? DEAR?

NO, JUST MORE PAD THAI LASAGNE PLEASE

RAMEN — POOR

25 PACKS FOR A BUCK? INFLATION SUCKS!

"SPECIAL SAUCE" — ANGRY

EVERY TIME I COME HERE I SAY "NO SAUCE"! AND EVERY TIME YOU IGNORE ME!!!

ICE CREAM — DELUSIONAL

I'LL EXERCISE THIS OFF TOMORROW.

CANNED SOUP — SUICIDAL

IT'S REALLY QUIET HERE SINCE SHE LEFT.

STIR STIR STIR ...

FAST FOOD — PARANOID

WHAT'S THIS SALTY, SLIMY STUFF?

SUSHI — INCOMPETENT

MAY I HAVE A FORK INSTEAD OF CHOPSTICKS?

OF COURSE. SHALL I FEED YOU AS WELL?

ARSENIC — LIBERATED

THIS STEAK BETTER BE TASTIER THAN THE CRAP YOU MADE YESTERDAY.

I ADDED SOMETHING EXTRA.

DEAR TINY,
HOW CAN I GET MY BOYFRIEND TO TELL HIS PARENTS I EXIST? THEY MAY DISAPPROVE AND HE'S AFRAID OF THAT. IT'S BEEN UNDER FOUR YEARS NOW AND I'M STILL INVISIBLE.
— GHOST GIRL
SEATTLE, WA

PERHAPS HIS PARENTS WOULD BE MORE ACCEPTING OF YOU IF YOU ARRANGED FOR THEM TO MEET HIS "OTHER GIRLFRIENDS" FIRST.

MY SENTENCE WAS REDUCED BECAUSE MY EX SURVIVED THE BLAZE.

BUT I'M ALL THROUGH WITH HEROIN. NOW I JUST DO METH.

IT WAS HARD BUT I FINALLY GOT IT DOWN TO ONE BOTTLE OF GIN A DAY.

I STILL LIVE WITH MY HUSBAND.

THANK YOU, A LOT OF PEOPLE TELL ME I LOOK LIKE A WOMAN.

I DON'T BELIEVE IN HYGIENE.

I ALREADY HAVE 8 KIDS FROM 3 OTHER MEN, BUT MAYBE YOU'LL BE GRANDPARENTS SOON.

Dear Tiny,
IS IT SMART FOR WOMEN TO PLAY GAMES ON MEN THEY LUST AFTER?
—WENDY
GREENWOOD, WA

I'M NOT SURE IF IT'S "SMART," BUT HERE ARE A FEW GAMES THAT ARE POPULAR.

"MONOPOLY"
...THEN AFTER THE FILM WE CAN VISIT MY MOM, THEN SPEND THE NIGHT AT YOUR PLACE. AND TOMORROW WE WILL...

"TRIVIAL PURSUIT"
REMEMBER WHAT TODAY IS SWEETIE?
THINK, THINK

"MOTHER MAY I"
WHY ARE YOU SO MAD? I TOLD YOU I'D BE WITH MY FRIENDS TONIGHT.
YOU DIDN'T ASK ME.

"HIDE AND SEEK"
...PLEASE LEAVE YOUR MESSAGE AFTER THE TONE. BEEEEP... IT'S ME AGAIN. WHY WON'T YOU CALL? WHERE ARE YOU? I JUST WANT TO TALK. PLEASE CALL.

"CHARADES"
WHAT'S WRONG? WHY WON'T YOU TELL ME? WHY ARE YOU SO QUIET?

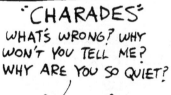

OF COURSE THESE GAMES COULD LEAD TO ONE YOU'D BETTER GET USED TO.

"SOLITAIRE"
WHY WON'T HE CALL?

DEAR TINY,
 I'M A "NICE GUY" BUT I DON'T SEEM TO ATTRACT ANY WOMEN. WHY IS THAT? WHAT DO WOMEN FIND SO SEDUCTIVE ABOUT JERKS?   — STEVE
                        SEATTLE, WA

HIS COLD, PASSIONLESS, NONCOMMUNICATIVE NATURE HAS ITS OWN CHARM.

I'VE GROWN TO ENJOY STAYING IN EVERY NIGHT AND WATCHING ALL HIS FAVORITE SHOWS.

DRINKING IS HIS WAY OF GETTING IN TOUCH WITH HIS FEELINGS. HE IS VERY COMPLEX.

NOW THAT HE WON'T ALLOW ME TO SEE MY FRIENDS AND FAMILY I CAN FOCUS ON MAKING OUR RELATIONSHIP BETTER.

HE MAY BE UNFAITHFUL, BUT HE LOVES ONLY ME.

HE POINTS OUT MY FAULTS AND INSECURITIES IN FRONT OF OTHERS, AND I'M A MUCH BETTER PERSON FOR IT.

HE NEEDS ME. HE DOESN'T HAVE A JOB SO HOW ELSE WILL HE PAY OFF ALL HIS BILLS?

HE DOES HAVE A QUICK TEMPER AND AN ABUSIVE PERSONALITY, BUT THAT WILL CHANGE WHEN THE BABY IS BORN.

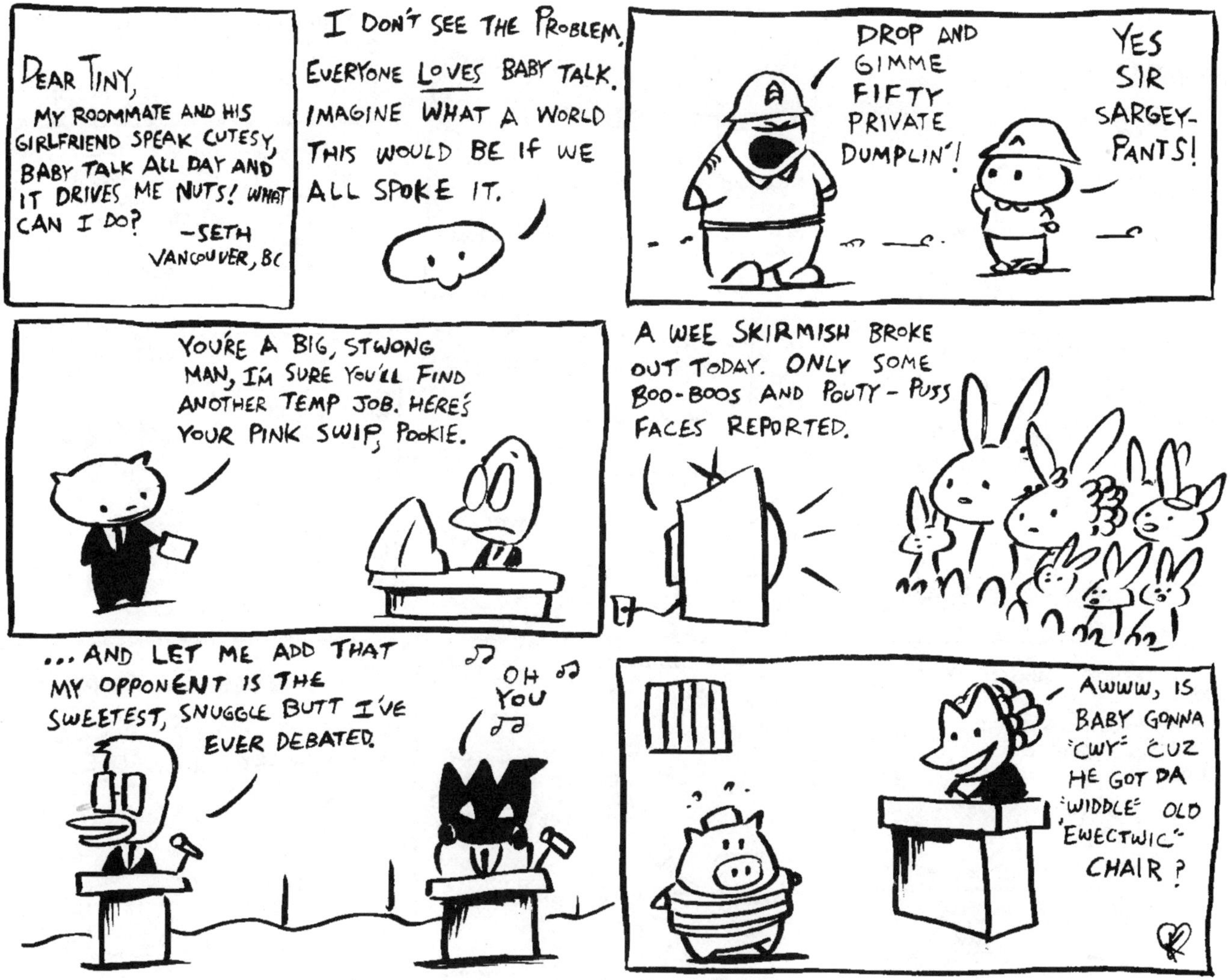
DEAR TINY,
MY ROOMMATE AND HIS GIRLFRIEND SPEAK CUTESY, BABY TALK ALL DAY AND IT DRIVES ME NUTS! WHAT CAN I DO?
—SETH
VANCOUVER, BC
I DON'T SEE THE PROBLEM. EVERYONE LOVES BABY TALK. IMAGINE WHAT A WORLD THIS WOULD BE IF WE ALL SPOKE IT.
DROP AND GIMME FIFTY PRIVATE DUMPLIN'!
YES SIR SARGEY-PANTS!
YOU'RE A BIG, STWONG MAN, I'M SURE YOU'LL FIND ANOTHER TEMP JOB. HERE'S YOUR PINK SWIP, POOKIE.
A WEE SKIRMISH BROKE OUT TODAY. ONLY SOME BOO-BOOS AND POUTY-PUSS FACES REPORTED.
...AND LET ME ADD THAT MY OPPONENT IS THE SWEETEST, SNUGGLE BUTT I'VE EVER DEBATED.
OH YOU
AWWW, IS BABY GONNA "CWY" CUZ HE GOT DA "WIDDLE" OLD "EWECTWIC" CHAIR?

Dear Tiny Sepuku,
How do you pick out a wedding ring?
— Tor
Seattle, WA

Tiny Sepuku's "Seven"
Simple Suggestions in Selecting a Wedding Ring"

① "Consider what it will be made out of. Gold, silver, titanium..."

...But it's "gold plated" plastic babe!

② "Be traditional, use a cherished family heirloom."

Man! Grandma sure had small fingers.

RIP

③ "Give careful thought to how you want your ring designed."

Look, mine has a skull and yours has a secret cyanide compartment.

Good.

④ "Shop around"

I wear this ring on my what?!

TOYS UNLTD

⑤ "Measure yourself carefully."

Looks like I need a really small ring.

Oh, I could have told you that.

⑥ "Choose a ring that symbolizes your eternal commitment."

I told you, I don't wear it at work or when I get drinks with the guys because I don't want to lose it. You mean that much to me baby.

⑦ "Consider resale value."

Is this enough as a retainer?

DIVORCE LAWYER

I JUST GOT A GREAT JOB OFFER IN ANOTHER CITY BUT MY GIRLFRIEND LIVES HERE AND DOESN'T WANT TO MOVE. HELP!

—JACK
ALBUQUERQUE, NM

39

Dear Tiny,
Let's say the guy you want has a girlfriend. How can I scare her off?

— Princess
Seattle, WA

① SPECULATE ON WHY THEY ARE TOGETHER.

So you two are going out? He must have quit drinking again.

Oh?

② ALLUDE TO HIS PRIOR RELATIONSHIPS.

I'm happy you two are an item. It's much healthier than all those hookers he used to frequent.

③ ASK ABOUT HIS PRE-EXISTING HEALTH CONDITION.

So I heard you can't even see his warts there anymore. Is that true?

Eew.

④ MENTION HOW MUCH YOU ADMIRE HER.

You're so strong to date a recovering crack addict and felon.

⑤ ONCE YOU HAVE HIM, WATCH YOUR BACK.

You hid a camera in my shower and put me on the net?!!!

But ALL the girls said you'd get turned on by it.

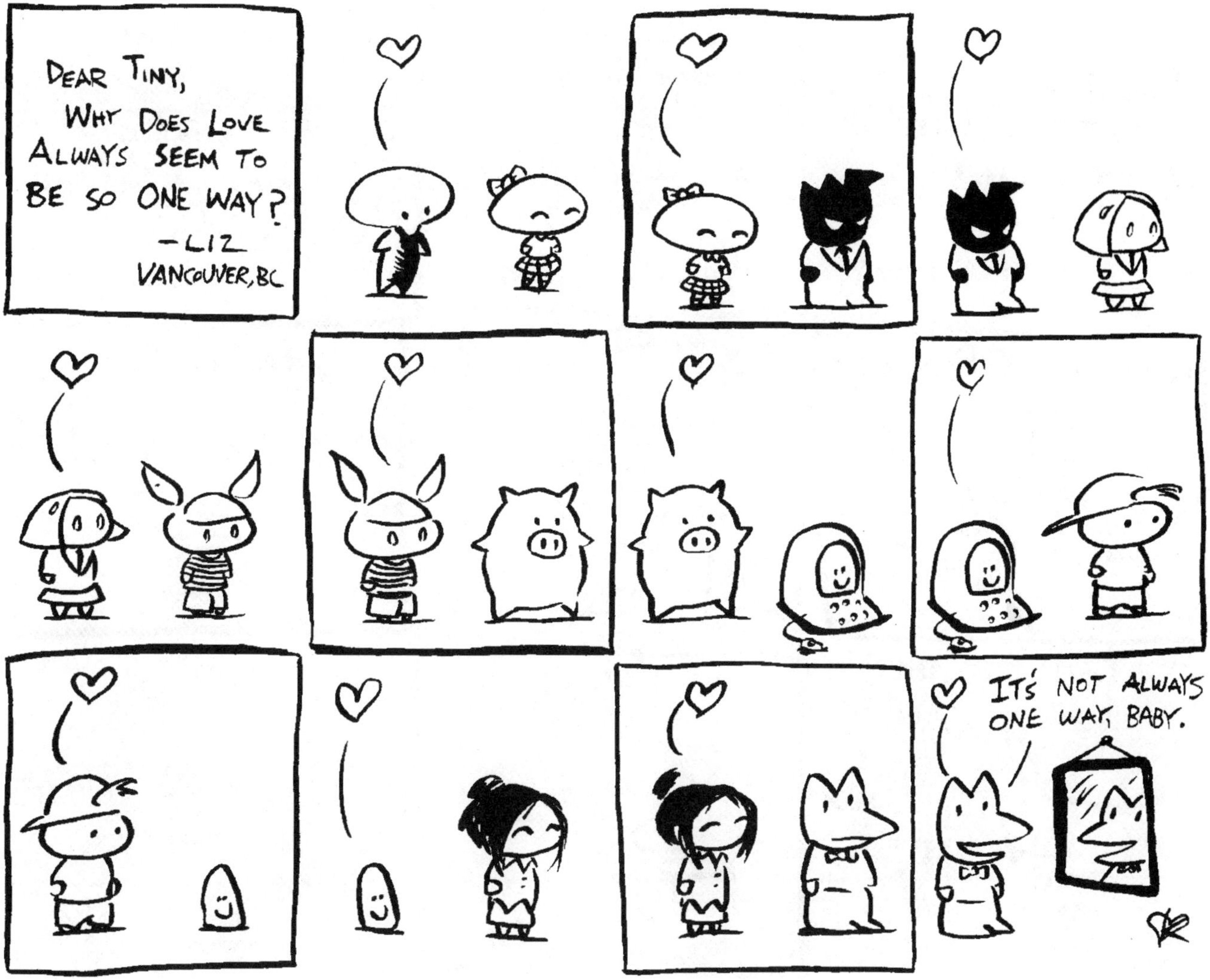
DEAR TINY,
WHY DOES LOVE ALWAYS SEEM TO BE SO ONE WAY?
-LIZ
VANCOUVER, BC
IT'S NOT ALWAYS ONE WAY, BABY.

DEAR TINY,
   WHAT SHOULD I GET MY
"EX" FOR "EX"-MAS?
            —D
   SEATTLE, WA

FRAMED PHOTO OF YOU AND YOUR NEW LOVER.

FAST FOOD COUPONS.

MOUTHWASH AND DEODORANT.

"WISH YOU WERE HERE" CARD FROM YOUR WINTER HOUSE ON MAUI.

VIAGRA.

OLD PHOTOS OF THEM.

S.T.D. TEST KIT.

FRUITCAKE.

42

DEAR TINY,
  I'VE HEARD A LOT OF HYPE
ABOUT THE YEAR 2000, BUT
HOW MUCH WILL OUR LIVES
REALLY CHANGE?   —TOM
              SEATTLE, WA

FLYING CARS!

ROBOTS!

GET A JOB!

SIX FINGERS!

I FAIL TO SEE ITS EVOLUTIONARY IMPACT.

THE NEW ICE AGE!

IT'S WARMER TODAY.

ALIEN COLONISTS!

OH, THAT'S NOTHING NEW.

CLONES!

MUTANTS!

NEW "LOVE" ORGANS!

WHERE'D THAT COME FROM?

DEAR TINY,
  HOW DO YOU STOP FROM
DREAMING ABOUT AN
EX-LOVER?   — BECKY
          SANTA CRUZ, CA

COFFEE

CHRONIC INSOMNIA

CRAMMING

SOLITAIRE

WELL...
JUST ONE
MORE GAME...

CHAT ROOMS

IT'S 5:00 AM HERE,
WHAT TIME IS IT
          THERE?

DREAM SUPPRESSANTS

THERE MAY
BE SOME
SIDE EFFECTS
THOUGH.

GEE, YA
THINK?

TRUCKIN'

I GOT 20 HOURS
AND 2000 MILES
TO GO.

"WAKE UP" MONKEY®

QUIT POKING!
I'M UP! I'M UP!

DEAR TINY,

EVER SINCE MY GIRLFRIEND LEFT ME I FIND MYSELF MORE INFLUENCED BY SEXY COMMERCIALS. AM I WEAK OR IS MY LONELINESS BEING TAKEN ADVANTAGE OF?

—TRENT
SEATTLE, WA

WHY AREN'T RISQUÉ METHODS USED TO PROMOTE MORE IMPORTANT THINGS?

CHARITY AUCTIONS

WHAT IS MY BID FOR THIS STACK OF NUDIE MAGAZINES?

CULTURAL ESTABLISHMENTS

ART MUSEUM

NOW MORE NUDES!

FINANCIAL PLANNING

MY RETIREMENT FUND IS TIED UP MOSTLY IN STRIP CLUBS AND ADULT FILM STUDIOS.

YOU SHOULD INVEST IN PORN SITES.

ACADEMICS

WE NOW OFFER FREE LAP DANCES TO STUDENTS WITH A G.P.A. OF 4.0.

SOCIAL CAUSES

PROTEST RALLY

NO!

STOP

AND "HOT BOD" CONTEST TONIGHT!!!

PLEDGE DRIVES

OUR VOLUNTEER PHONE SEX OPERATORS ARE WAITING FOR YOUR CALLS.

HOLY MOLY! WHERE'S MY CREDIT CARD!

POLITICAL DEBATES

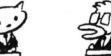

I'D LIKE TO GIVE MY REBUTTAL IN THE FORM OF A STRIP-TEASE.

Dear Tiny,
My last three dates have been disasters. Is there any way I can make a guy reveal his true personality before I commit to a date?
— Lisa

There are lots of different clues to reveal personality traits. Pets can tell a lot about their owners.

CATS

MEW?

YES?

MYSTERIOUS

DOGS

DADDY IS HOME! HOW'S MY BOY DOIN'?

BOW WOW WOW

PATERNAL

VENUS FLYTRAP

THAT'S RIGHT, FLY, SEAL YOUR OWN FATE.

PASSIVE AGGRESSIVE

NANO-PET

UH-OH. IS BABY HUNGRY?

BEEP BEEP BEEP

ARRESTED DEVELOPMENT

ANT FARM

BEHOLD A WHOLE CIVILIZATION DEPENDENT UPON ME!

MEGALOMANIACAL TENDENCIES

SEA-MONKEY

WAIT... THESE AREN'T MONKEYS!

NAIVE

PET ROCK

LOVE ME!

BONK

OW!

INTIMACY ISSUES

DEAR TINY,

WHAT DO GUYS HOPE TO ACHIEVE BY HONKING AT YOU FROM THEIR CAR?

— MARYANNE
DALLAS, TX

IT'S THE MOST RECENT EVOLUTIONARY STEP IN HUMAN MATING CALLS.

CAVEMEN USED VERBAL BEEPS AND CHEST POUNDING TO ATTRACT MATES.

BEEP!
BEEP!
THUMPA! THUMPA!

EGYPTIAN PHAROAHS USED THOUSANDS OF SLAVES TO BEEP DURING COURTSHIP.

BEEP!

THE INCANS USED TO TRAIN MONKEYS TO BEEP

EEP! EEP!

ANCIENT CHINESE USED BEEPING FIREWORKS.

BEEP!

THE SWISS DEVELOPED HORNS TO BEEP ACROSS GREAT DISTANCES.

BEEP!

MODERN MAN NOW USES CAR HORNS TO TRY AND ATTRACT WOMEN JUST AS THEIR ANCESTORS DID...

BEEP BEEP!

...STILL ELICITING THE SAME TIMELESS RESPONSE FROM THEM AEONS LATER.

IDIOT.

Dear Tiny,

I'm really awkward around women, especially when I try to flirt with them. Do you have any advice I can use to be better at it?

— Richard
Dallas, TX

Flirting is hard for shy guys. But try this.

Be more approachable. Wear an inviting and relaxed smile. Observe:

If a woman is interested she'll respond with a look like this:

But you should leave her alone if she looks at you like this:

I hope that makes flirting a little less confusing than it already is.

DEAR TINY,

MY, EX-BOYFRIEND STILL CALLS ME EVERY NOW AND THEN. THE THING IS HE ALWAYS ENDS UP PICKING A FIGHT OR TRYING TO IRRITATE ME. I'M SURE THAT HE DOESN'T WANT US TO GET BACK TOGETHER, SO WHY MUST HE DO THIS? —MONIQUE NEW MEXICO

MY FRIEND HERE KEEPS IN TOUCH WITH HIS "EXES," PERHAPS HE CAN HELP YOU UNDERSTAND.

WELL, I COMPLAIN A LOT ABOUT ALL MY EX-GIRLFRIENDS

I DO THIS TO TURN MY FRIENDS, MY FAMILY, AND EVEN SOME OF THEIR FRIENDS AGAINST THEM.

I ALSO GET A LOT OF PITY DATES WHEN I COMPLAIN ABOUT FORMER LOVERS.

BUT ALL MY COMPLAINTS GET OLD QUICK.

SO I CALL UP MY OLD FLAMES AND ARGUE WITH THEM SO I'LL HAVE NEW STUFF TO COMPLAIN ABOUT.

WOULDN'T IT BE HEALTHIER IF YOU GREW UP A BIT AND MOVED ON?

WHAT? AND GIVE UP ALL THAT SWEET SYMPATHY BOOTY?

POOR THING. I'LL HELP YOU FORGET YOUR EVIL EX.

49

DEAR TINY,
 THERE'S THIS GIRL I LIKE BUT SHE ONLY DATES OLDER GUYS. WHAT CAN I DO TO GET HER ATTENTION?
— JEFF

I'M NOT EXACTLY SURE HOW OLD YOU ARE, BUT I HAVE HAD THE SAME PROBLEM SINCE I WAS IN JR. HIGH.

BACK THEN THE GIRLS I LIKED DATED HIGH SCHOOL GUYS.

WHEN I GOT TO HIGH SCHOOL THEY DATED COLLEGE BOYS.

IN COLLEGE THEY WENT AFTER GRAD STUDENTS.

IN GRAD SCHOOL THEY HAD A THING FOR PROFESSORS.

AT WORK THEY'D BE FLIRTING WITH THE SENIOR EXECUTIVES.

SO NOW I'VE REACHED THIS POINT WHERE THE GUYS WHO ATTRACT THE WOMEN I LIKE AREN'T OLDER THAN ME ANYMORE. BUT I'M STILL HAVING THE SAME PROBLEM I HAD IN JR. HIGH...

... HIGH SCHOOL GUYS.

THAT NEW TEEN BOY BAND IS SO YUMMY!

MY BAG BOY HAS THE HOTTEST BOD.

PRINCE WILLIAM IS A CUTIE!

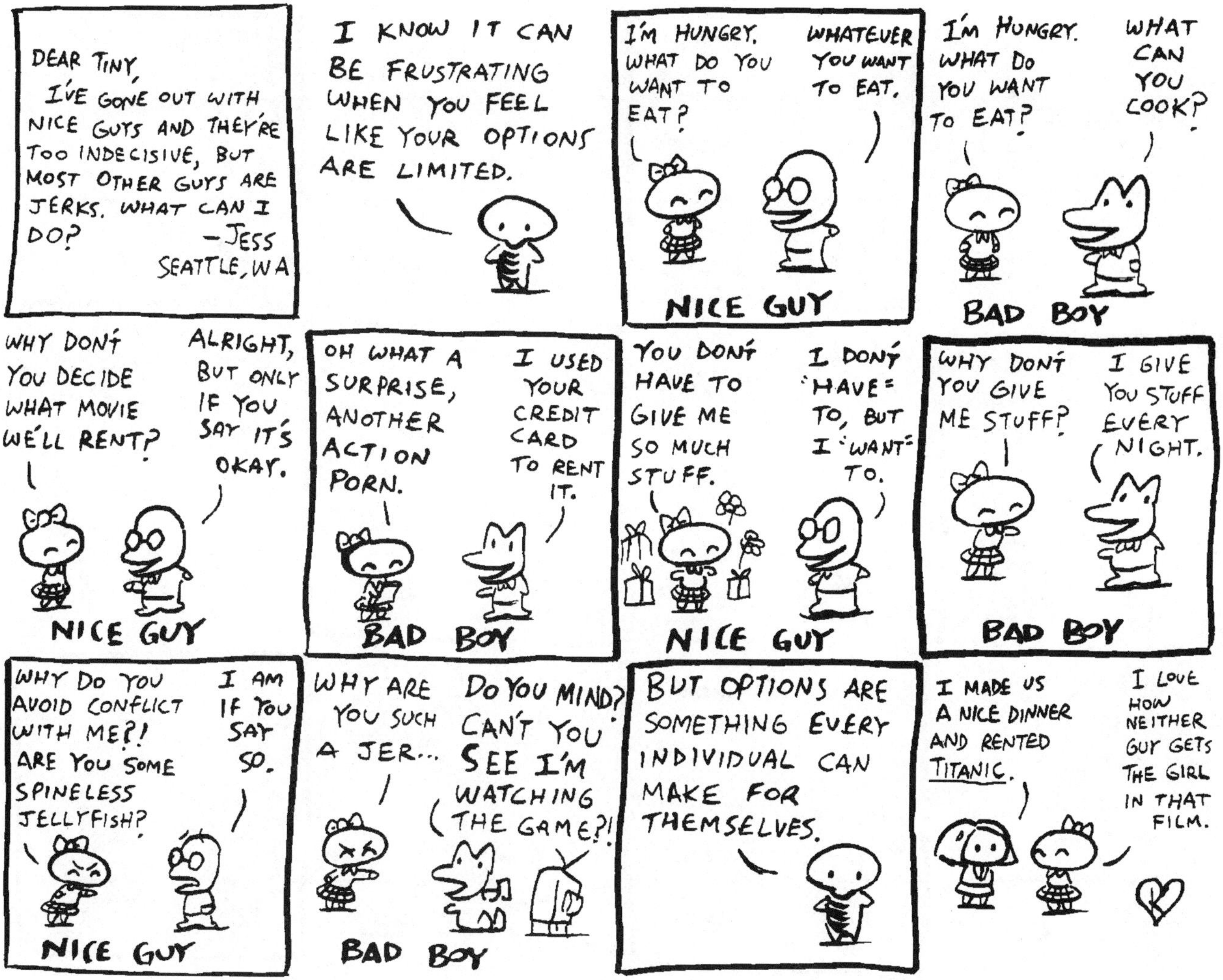
DEAR TINY,
I'VE GONE OUT WITH NICE GUYS AND THEY'RE TOO INDECISIVE, BUT MOST OTHER GUYS ARE JERKS. WHAT CAN I DO?
—JESS SEATTLE, WA
I KNOW IT CAN BE FRUSTRATING WHEN YOU FEEL LIKE YOUR OPTIONS ARE LIMITED.
I'M HUNGRY. WHAT DO YOU WANT TO EAT?
WHATEVER YOU WANT TO EAT.
NICE GUY
I'M HUNGRY. WHAT DO YOU WANT TO EAT?
WHAT CAN YOU COOK?
BAD BOY
WHY DON'T YOU DECIDE WHAT MOVIE WE'LL RENT?
ALRIGHT, BUT ONLY IF YOU SAY IT'S OKAY.
NICE GUY
OH WHAT A SURPRISE, ANOTHER ACTION PORN.
I USED YOUR CREDIT CARD TO RENT IT.
BAD BOY
YOU DON'T HAVE TO GIVE ME SO MUCH STUFF.
I DON'T "HAVE" TO, BUT I "WANT" TO.
NICE GUY
WHY DON'T YOU GIVE ME STUFF?
I GIVE YOU STUFF EVERY NIGHT.
BAD BOY
WHY DO YOU AVOID CONFLICT WITH ME?! ARE YOU SOME SPINELESS JELLYFISH?
I AM IF YOU SAY SO.
NICE GUY
WHY ARE YOU SUCH A JER...
DO YOU MIND? CAN'T YOU SEE I'M WATCHING THE GAME?!
BAD BOY
BUT OPTIONS ARE SOMETHING EVERY INDIVIDUAL CAN MAKE FOR THEMSELVES.
I MADE US A NICE DINNER AND RENTED TITANIC.
I LOVE HOW NEITHER GUY GETS THE GIRL IN THAT FILM.

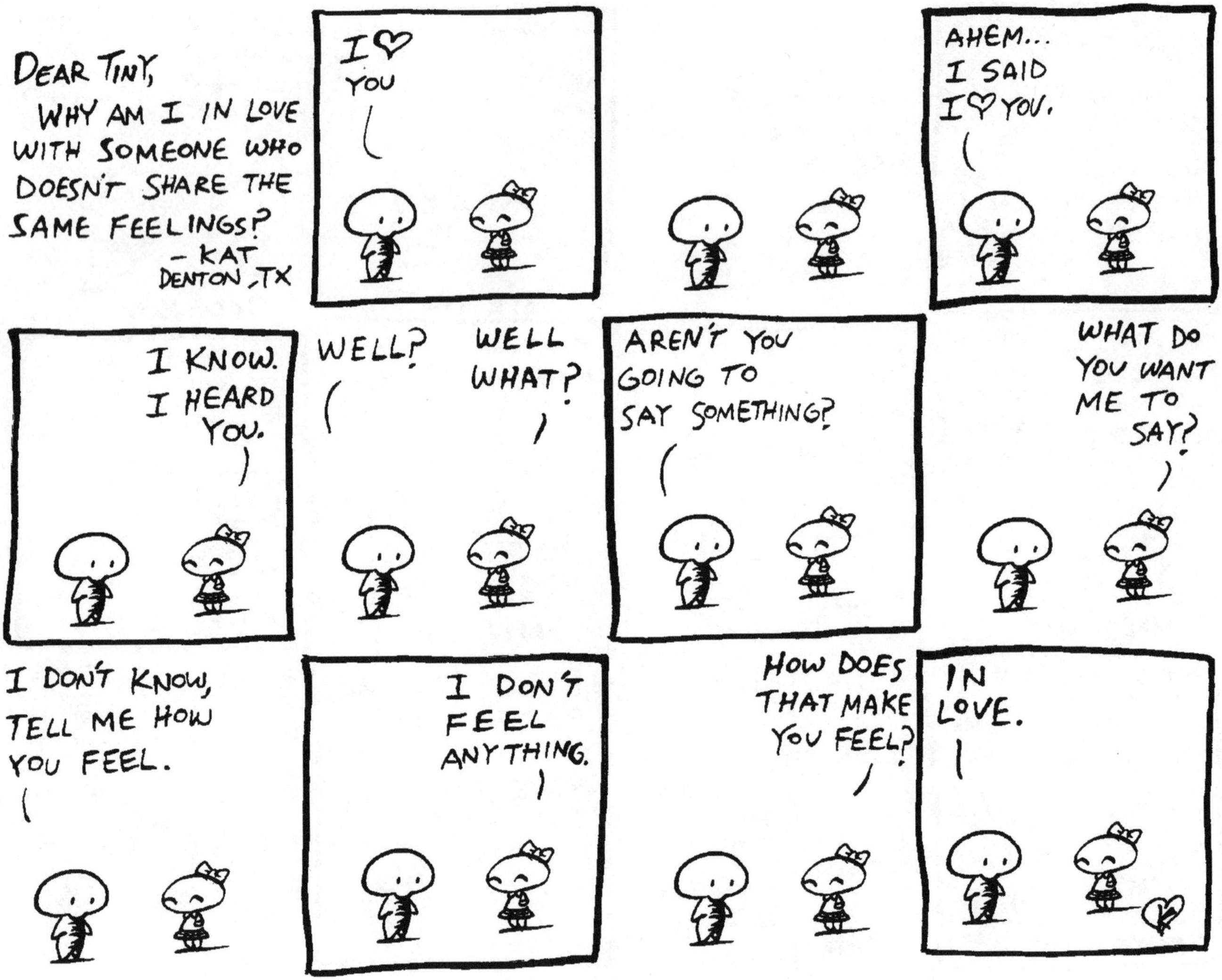
DEAR TINY,
WHY AM I IN LOVE WITH SOMEONE WHO DOESN'T SHARE THE SAME FEELINGS?
- KAT
DENTON, TX
I ♡ YOU
AHEM... I SAID I ♡ YOU.
I KNOW. I HEARD YOU.
WELL?
WELL WHAT?
AREN'T YOU GOING TO SAY SOMETHING?
WHAT DO YOU WANT ME TO SAY?
I DON'T KNOW, TELL ME HOW YOU FEEL.
I DON'T FEEL ANYTHING.
HOW DOES THAT MAKE YOU FEEL?
IN LOVE.

DEAR TINY,

CAN YOU TELL ME WHERE ALL THE COOL, INTERESTING, FUNKY GUYS HANG OUT? I DON'T HAVE A LOT OF CASH, SO CLUBS ARE A LUXURY.

—ELIZABETH, WA

WHY GO FIND THEM? HERE ARE SOME WAYS YOU CAN LEAD THEM TO YOU AND MAYBE SUPPLEMENT YOUR INCOME.

STAND-UP COMEDY

IF MY SELF EFFACING WIT DOESN'T ATTRACT 'EM, THEN MY BITTER TAKE ON ROMANCE DEFINITELY WILL.

♫ BA-DUM-BUMP

INDIE COMIC BOOK ARTIST

'CUZ THOSE COMICONS ARE HUNK FESTS.

OPEN MIC POET

A PROPER HAIKU HAS 17 SYLLABLES MINE'S NO EXCEPTION

SNAP   SNAP
SNAP
SNAP   SNAP

MUSICIAN

YOU WANT TO BOOK A SHOW WITH ME?

YEAH, IT'S A SMALL VENUE IN MY ROOM.

LEAD A "MEN'S GROUP"

GRRR.

THUMPA THUMPA THUMPA

GRUNT

SNORT

PERFORMANCE ART

OKAY EVERYONE, START TOSSING THE EGGS AT ME.

THROW A RAVE

UH... IS THERE ANYONE HERE OLD ENOUGH TO DRIVE?

53

DEAR TINY,
WHEN I TOLD MY GIRLFRIEND THAT A FRIEND HAD KISSED ME UNEXPECTEDLY AND WITHOUT MY PERMISSION SHE SAID I HAD BEEN UNFAITHFUL, EVEN THOUGH I DIDN'T WANT THE KISS. IS SHE RIGHT?
— RICH BO
SEATTLE, WA

I HAVE NEVER HAD THAT KIND OF EXPERIENCE.

BUT MY FRIEND HERE HAS.

HOW DID YOU HANDLE THE SITUATION?

WELL, I HAD MY FRIEND WHO KISSED ME TELL MY GIRLFRIEND WHAT HAPPENED.

SHE TOLD HER IT WAS A HARMLESS LITTLE THING.

THEN, WITHOUT ANY WARNING, SHE KISSES MY GIRLFRIEND TO SHOW HER HOW INNOCENT IT WAS.

AND THAT SAVED YOUR RELATIONSHIP?

...WELL, NOT EXACTLY.

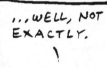

Dear Tiny,
   I WANT TO MARRY
A MULTIMILLIONAIRE!
                  — CHRIS
              SAN DIEGO, CA

HERE ARE A FEW ELIGIBLE TYCOONS THAT DIDN'T MAKE THE CUT FOR THE T.V. SHOW.

SLUMLORD

RENT DOUBLES FOR TOILETS.

INSIDE TRADER

I WORK FOR "TIPS."

PORNOGRAPHER

I PROMISE YOU THAT EVERYONE WILL WANT TO SEE OUR WEDDING PICTURES.

CULT LEADER

MY WIVES AND I WELCOME YOU TO THE FAMILY.

SMUGGLER

PACK LIGHT, WE'LL BE BRINGING A LOT OF STUFF HOME FROM OUR HONEYMOON IN COLUMBIA.

COUNTERFEITER

MILLIONAIRE? BABY I'M A FREAKIN' ZILLIONAIRE!

IMPOSTER

WHAT DO YOU MEAN NONE OF THE CONTESTANTS ARE MILLIONAIRESSES?

DEAR TINY,
MY GIRLFRIEND SAYS SHE WANTS ME TO BE HONEST WITH HER, BUT IT SEEMS LIKE I'M ALWAYS GETTING IN ARGUMENTS WITH HER WHEN I AM. WHAT CAN I DO?
— LOGAN
SAN DIMAS, CA

YOU CAN STILL TELL THE TRUTH (JUST NOT THE ENTIRE TRUTH).

DO I LOOK FAT?

NO... (FATTER).

WHAT DID YOU LIKE BEST ABOUT YOUR EX?

NOTHING (I WILL EVER TELL YOU).

SO, SIZE DOESN'T MATTER?

DON'T BE SILLY (STUBBY).

IF I WAS HORRIBLY DISFIGURED IN AN ACCIDENT, WOULD YOU STILL LOVE ME?

OF COURSE (NOT).

SO HOW MANY WERE BEFORE ME?

ONLY A FEW (DOZEN).

DO YOU THINK SHE'S MORE ATTRACTIVE THAN ME?

NO (SHE IS DEFINITELY MORE ATTRACTIVE).

I JUST DREW IT. WHAT DO YA THINK?

IT'S FUNNY (HOW YOU MANAGE TO SELL THIS CRAP).

Dear Tiny,
Why is it that every person that seems to be a "sure thing" turns out to be the complete opposite, and those who you don't give the slightest thought to work out so well?

— Christina

I LIKE YOU...

...BUT I'M ATTRACTED TO YOU.

I KNOW YOUR LOVE IS SINCERE AND YOU CARE...

... BUT THAT DOESN'T APPEAL TO ME.

I KNOW YOU'LL USE ME AND TREAT ME LIKE A FOOL...

...YET I DESIRE TO BE WITH YOU MORE THAN ANYTHING.

SO I GUESS I'LL GIVE MYSELF TO YOU.

AND I'LL KEEP YOU AS A BACKUP, BECAUSE I KNOW YOU'LL WAIT.

EVEN THOUGH I HAVE FEELINGS FOR ALMOST EVERYONE BUT YOU.

I WILL NEED THAT TYPE OF DEVOTION WHEN I GET TIRED OF GIVING MY HEART TO THE WRONG PEOPLE.

YEAH, I KNOW THE FEELING.

DEAR TINY,

I'VE ASKED THIS GUY OUT 3 TIMES AND HE EITHER SAYS "MAYBE" OR JUST DOESN'T CALL. HE MAKES ME SO NERVOUS. AM I BEING TOO AGGRESSIVE BY CALLING SOMEONE I CAN'T TALK TO IN PERSON?
—ELEANOR
SEATTLE, WA

WHAT ARE YOU DOING?

WAITING FOR A CALL.

SO HE SAID HE'D CALL TODAY?

WELL... HE SAID MAYBE.

AND YOU EQUATE "MAYBE" WITH "YES"?

WHY? DO YOU THINK THAT'S NAIVE?

MAYBE.

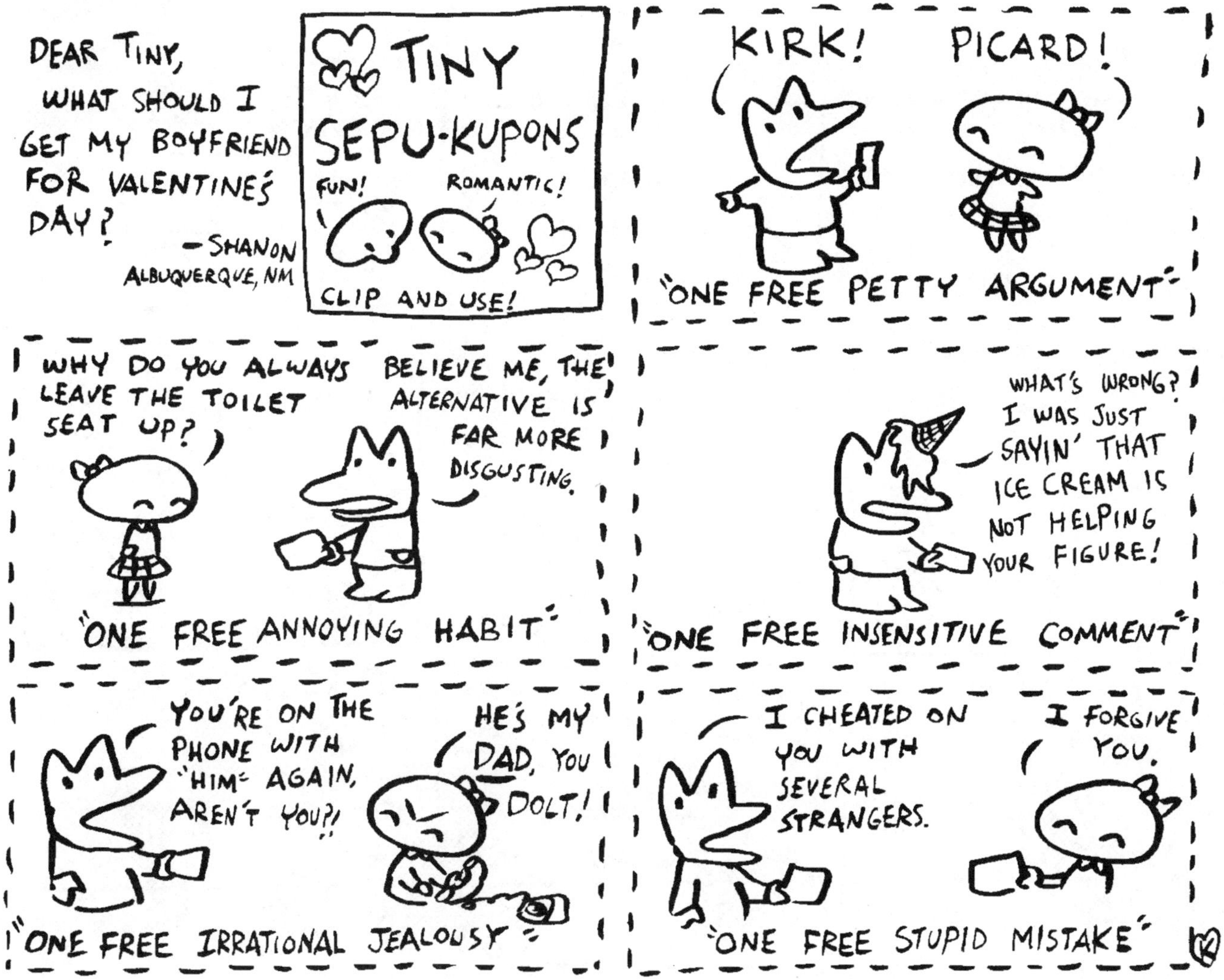
DEAR TINY,
WHAT SHOULD I GET MY BOYFRIEND FOR VALENTINE'S DAY?
—SHANON
ALBUQUERQUE, NM
TINY
SEPU-KUPONS
FUN!
ROMANTIC!
CLIP AND USE!
KIRK!
PICARD!
"ONE FREE PETTY ARGUMENT"
WHY DO YOU ALWAYS LEAVE THE TOILET SEAT UP?
BELIEVE ME, THE ALTERNATIVE IS FAR MORE DISGUSTING.
"ONE FREE ANNOYING HABIT"
WHAT'S WRONG? I WAS JUST SAYIN' THAT ICE CREAM IS NOT HELPING YOUR FIGURE!
"ONE FREE INSENSITIVE COMMENT"
YOU'RE ON THE PHONE WITH "HIM" AGAIN, AREN'T YOU?!
HE'S MY DAD, YOU DOLT!
"ONE FREE IRRATIONAL JEALOUSY"
I CHEATED ON YOU WITH SEVERAL STRANGERS.
I FORGIVE YOU.
"ONE FREE STUPID MISTAKE"

DEAR TINY,
I JUST STARTED CLUBBING AND I'M BEING HIT ON BY REAL SLEAZES. HOW CAN I KEEP THEM AWAY?
— CHRIS
VANCOUVER, BC

① REPLY TO THEIR EFFORTS USING A SINGULAR NONSENSICAL WORD.

GRONK!
GRONK!
GRONK!

② BE HONEST

AS TEMPTING AS IT IS TO GREATLY LOWER MY DATING STANDARDS FOR YOU, I'M GONNA HAVE TO PASS.

③ BE CANDID.

... I THOUGHT THOSE SORES WOULD NEVER STOP ITCHING.

④ AS THEY ARE SPEAKING, CROSS YOUR EYES AND SAY "DUH" A LOT.

DUH...
UH...
DUH...
"SNIFF"...
DU-UH

?

⑤ ANSWER THEM SPEAKING IN A ROBOT VOICE.

THANK YOU FOR THE DRINH HUMAN.

WHAT IS IT WITH THE LADIES HERE?

⑥ LET THEM IN ON YOUR LITTLE SECRET.

YOU DO KNOW I'M A GUY, RIGHT?

⑦ BE OVERLY COMFORTABLE AROUND HIM.

WOOO! I SHOULDN'T HAVE EATEN SO MANY ENCHILADAS.

I'LL SAY!

⑧ BE ASSERTIVE.

AHHH!!! MY EYES! THEY BURN!

60

DEAR TINY
THERE IS THIS GIRL I'VE BEEN
THINKING ABOUT, BUT WE LOST TOUCH
LONG AGO. I DON'T KNOW WHERE
SHE IS OR HOW TO REACH HER OR
EVEN IF SHE WANTS TO HEAR FROM
ME. WHAT CAN I DO?
— CONFUSED

WHENEVER I WANT TO GET
IN CONTACT WITH A LONG-
LOST FRIEND...

...I USE MENTAL
TELEPATHY!

IT'S A RELATIVELY EASY
PROCESS. IT JUST TAKES
PRACTICE.

FIRST CONCENTRATE ON THE
IMAGE OF THE PERSON YOU
ARE TRYING TO CONTACT.

THEN PICTURE YOURSELF
TRANSMITTING YOUR MESSAGE
DIRECTLY INTO THEIR MIND.

I'LL DEMONSTRATE. OBSERVE
AS I ATTEMPT TO CONTACT
A CHILDHOOD SWEETIE.

HOW COME YOU
ALWAYS GET THESE
HEADACHES WHEN
WE'RE TRYING TO
BE ALONE?

SHUT UP AND
GET ME SOME
ASPRIN!

DEAR TINY,
   HOW DO YOU FIGURE OUT WHAT
TO DO WITH FRIENDS THAT ARE
BOTH YOUR EX'S AND YOURS?
(I.E., AT PARTIES WHERE YOU'RE
BOTH INVITED OR EVEN E-MAILS
WHERE YOU'RE BOTH ON THE SAME
FWD LIST?)
                    —ANNA
                 SEATTLE, WA

HAVING MUTUAL FRIENDS WITH
AN EX IS A VERY AWKWARD
SITUATION. AND THAT'S NOT
EASY TO CHANGE.

SO I SAY MAKE IT AS
AWKWARD AS YOU CAN
FOR EVERYONE INVOLVED.

"GET DRUNK AND BLAB
LOUDLY ABOUT YOUR EX
AT PARTIES."

...AND IT LOOKS LIKE
A LITTLE STRAW
MUSHROOM! A
MUSHROOM! HA!!!
≡HIC≡

"BRING HOT DATES TO PARTIES."

THESE ARE
MY NEW
BOYFRIENDS.

OH...?

"OR HIT ON YOUR EX'S DATE."

YOU WANNA
DITCH THIS
PARTY?

SURE.

YOU TWO
GETTING
ALONG?

"REPLY TO EMAIL LISTS WITH
PICS OF YOU AND YOUR
NEW LOVER(S)."

ISN'T THAT
YOUR
GIRLFRIEND
AND YOUR
EX?

AND OF COURSE IF YOU
REALLY WANT TO MAKE
THINGS AWKWARD, TRY
THIS AT A PARTY...

WELL... I'D
BETTER GO.

I'M SO
CONFUSED...

HEY, AREN'T
YOU GUYS
BROKEN UP?

62

Dear Tiny,

When is it okay to talk to your ex again?

—Stacey
Kirkland, WA

Reestablishing contact with a former lover is a very delicate thing.

I've made a timetable to give you an idea of what to expect in a post-relationship meeting.

UNDER ONE MONTH

OH NO... WHOOPS...

MISTAKE

1-5 MONTHS LATER

MEET MY NEW BOYFRIEND. LET'S KISS IN FRONT OF HIM.

BIGGER MISTAKE

6-12 MONTHS

MY GIRLFRIEND IS CUTER THAN YOU. MY BOYFRIEND ISN'T A FAILURE.

MUTUAL ANIMOSITY

1-2 YEARS

I PLAY ALOOF, BUT I REALLY MISS YOU. I'LL SAY "KEEP IN TOUCH," BUT I WON'T MEAN IT.

DECEPTIVE PERIOD

3-9 YEARS

WHY DID WE BREAK UP? WE HAD SOME GOOD TIMES.

NOSTALGIC PERIOD

10 YEARS OR MORE

YOU HAVE 8 KIDS? WOW!! AND YOU "CAME OUT"?

CLEAN SLATE

63

DEAR TS,
   I'VE TRIED EVERYTHING AND CAN'T SEEM TO MEET THE LADIES. WHERE ARE ALL THE GOOD ONES HIDING? WHERE CAN I MEET THEM?

GENTLEMEN'S CLUBS

I DON'T HAVE A BUCK, BUT HERE'S A FLOWER.

GET LOST, CREEP!

FEMALE SELF-DEFENSE CLASS

YOU ALL WANT TO SPAR WITH ME? COOL!

LET ME KICK HIM FIRST.

SORORITIES

SO... YOU LADIES LOOKIN' FOR NEW PLEDGES?

CONVENT

WHY ALL THE BLACK? YOU CHICKS INTO GOTH OR SOMETHIN'?

LET ME KICK HIM FIRST.

LILITH FAIR

ANY OF YOU HONEYS KNOW IF KID ROCK OR EMINEM ARE GONNA PLAY?

GET OUT!

LESBIAN BAR

YOU DIDN'T NEED TO PEPPER SPRAY ME!!!

I TOLD YOU TO STOP STARING AT US, BUDDY.

GYNECOLOGIST'S OFFICE

IT'S MY FIRST VISIT.

I THINK YOU WANT THE PSYCHIATRIST DOWN THE HALL.

LADIES' ROOM

I CAN EXPLAIN, OFFICER.

DEAR TINY,
  I JUST LOST MY JOB AND I FEEL LESS ATTRACTIVE TO WOMEN NOW. WHAT CAN I DO?

  — ADAM
    DALLAS, TX

TURN YOUR MISFORTUNE INTO Ms. FORTUNE!

THANKS TO A BOOMING ECONOMY THERE ARE MORE WEALTHY WOMEN OUT THERE THAN EVER BEFORE.

YAY!

SOME OF THEM FLEX THEIR FINANCIAL MUSCLE AS "SUGAR MAMAS."

NOW I CAN CONTROL BOYS WITH MY LOOKS AND MY CASH. SWEET!

YOU CAN CASH IN ON THESE LADIES IF YOU PLAY THEIR WAY.

YOU'LL WEAR THIS COLLAR, CALL ME MA'AM, AND DO EVERYTHING I TELL YOU.

OF COURSE, YOU CAN ALWAYS JUST GET A NEW JOB.

YOU'LL WEAR A TIE, CALL ME SIR, AND DO WHAT I SAY.

DEAR TINY,
MY EX SAID SHE WANTED TO BE FRIENDS AFTER WE BROKE UP, BUT SHE DOESN'T PUT ANY EFFORT INTO MAINTAINING OUR FRIEND- SHIP. WHY DOES SHE DO THIS?
— SEAN

I WANT TO BREAK UP, BUT WE CAN STILL BE FRIENDS.

AFTER ALL WE'VE MEANT TO EACH OTHER WE SHOULD STILL KEEP IN CONTACT.

SO YOU STILL WANT TO HANG OUT WITH ME?

WELL...NOT TOO MUCH... IN FACT HARDLY AT ALL

CAN I CALL YOU UP?

SURE, BUT I'LL BE OUT A LOT WITH NEW GUYS SO DON'T EXPECT TO REACH ME.

HOW ABOUT E-MAIL?

ONLY IF IT'S LIMITED TO THOSE IMPERSONAL GROUP MAILINGS OF HILARIOUS JOKE LISTS.

SO YOU DON'T REALLY WANT A "FRIEND," YOU WANT A GUILT- FREE BREAKUP.

ALL MY BREAK- UPS ARE GUILT- FREE.

JUST ASK ALL MY "FRIENDS."

DEAR TINY,

WHAT IS A GIRL SUPPOSED TO DO WITH A REALLY SHY GUY SHE WANTS, BUT IS FRUSTRATED BY HIS ATTITUDE AND DOESN'T WANT TO SCARE HIM?

— WENDY
BALLARD, WA

LET'S TAKE A LOOK AT THE BASIC PSYCHOLOGICAL COMPONENTS THAT MAKE UP THE MIND OF A "SHY-BOY."

"AS YOU CAN SEE, "FEAR" IS A MAJOR INFLUENCE OVER THE SHY-BOY."

HE IS IN A PERPETUAL STATE OF FRIGHT, SO YOUR WORRIES ABOUT SCARING HIM OFF ARE UNFOUNDED. HE IS ALREADY AFRAID OF YOU.

BUT WITH THE CORRECT APPROACH, YOU CAN MAKE THIS WORK TO YOUR BENEFIT.

YOU'RE MY BOYFRIEND NOW!! GOT A PROBLEM WITH THAT?!

N-N-NO MA'AM.

Dear Tiny,

Why do men put such a high value on physical appearance with women?

— ABI
REDMOND, WA

MOST MEN TODAY ARE DESCENDANTS OF PREHISTORIC SHALLOW MEN.

YOU SEE, THERE WERE TWO TYPES OF CAVEMEN.

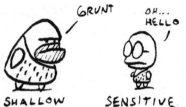

SHALLOW MAN WAS GUIDED BY HIS DESIRES TO PASS HIS GENES ON TO AS MANY ATTRACTIVE MATES AS POSSIBLE.

WHILE SENSITIVE MAN FOCUSED HIS AFFECTION ON ONE MATE AFTER A LONG COURTSHIP OF LEARNING ABOUT THEM.

AS A RESULT, SHALLOW MAN FLOODED THE GENE POOL WITH HIS PROGENY.

WHILE SENSITIVE MAN WAS USUALLY EATEN BY PREDATORS BEFORE HE COULD PROCREATE.

DESPITE THAT, A FEW OF THE SENSITIVE GENES SURVIVED TO PRESENT DAY.

WHICH IS GOOD BECAUSE WHO ELSE IS GOING TO RAISE SHALLOW MAN'S KIDS?

Dear Tiny,
   Does "Sepuku" mean anything?
                              — Suki

Yeah, what does "Sepuku" mean?

It's a Japanese word.

Essentially it means "self sacrifice for the benefit of others."

Like when a samurai gives up his life for the honor of his clan,

Or like when a mother tenaciously defends her young from a pack of stronger predators,

Or when a person loses their life while coming to the aid of a complete stranger.

So what does "Tiny" refer to?

Uh... Nothing. Never ask that question again!

DEAR TINY,
WHEN SHOULD I WORRY
ABOUT MY SELF-ESTEEM?
— AL
DALLAS, TX

NEXT TIME YOU GO
GROCERY SHOPPING,
ASK YOURSELF
THESE QUESTIONS,
AND MAYBE YOU
CAN BETTER DECIDE
IF YOU NEED
PROFESSIONAL HELP.

① DO YOU SHOP AFTER
MIDNIGHT?

NO CHANCE OF
MEETING ANYONE
DESIRABLE AT
THIS TIME.

② WHAT TYPE OF VEGGIES
DO YOU BUY?

WHY, I'LL GET
THIS BOTTLE OF
LIMP, SOFT PICKLES
OVER THIS FIRM,
VITAL CUCUMBER.

③ WHAT SECTION DO YOU
SPEND THE MOST TIME IN?

FINALLY. NOW
TO GET SOME
CORNFLAKES
FOR THIS.

XXX

④ WHAT PERIODICAL DO YOU
BUY FOR CURRENT EVENTS?

FRASIER
IS A
RERUN
AGAIN.

TV

⑤ WHAT DO YOU CONSIDER
THE FOUR FOOD GROUPS?

BEER
CANDY
SOUP
CIGS

⑥ DO YOU AVOID THE CUTE
CASHIER BECAUSE SHE IS
"OUT OF YOUR LEAGUE"?

I CAN HELP
YOU HERE,
SIR.

UH... NO
THANKS.

⑦ ARE YOU THREATENED
BY CANDY BAR SIZES?

KING SIZE?!
HOW AM I
S'POSED TO
COMPETE WITH
THAT?

DEAR TINY,
DOES EVERYBODY HAVE A "SOUL MATE"?
— "BEE"
SEATTLE, WA

TO HELP ANSWER YOUR QUESTION, I'VE ASKED THIS "SOUL MATE" TO BE MY GUEST.

SO, WHAT IS IT LIKE BEING A "SOUL MATE"?

PRETTY FREAKIN' SWEET!

I GET PLACED ON PEDESTALS AND I ALWAYS GET MY WAY.

I'M LAVISHED WITH ATTENTION AND AFFECTION FROM ADORING LOVERS.

BUT THE BEST PART IS ALL THE FREEDOM I HAVE.

I CAN SEE OTHER PEOPLE, ACT SELFISHLY AND IRRESPONSIBLY, EVEN BREAK UP WITH THEM.

AND THEY ALWAYS WAIT FAITHFULLY AND ALWAYS BLAME THEMSELVES FOR THE WAY I TREAT THEM.

THEN THEY BEG FOR ME TO RETURN BECAUSE "OUR LOVE WAS MEANT TO BE"! HA! HA!

UH... DOESN'T BEING A "SOUL MATE" REQUIRE YOU TO HAVE A SOUL?

WHAT DO YOU MEAN? I HAVE THEIRS.

71

DEAR TINY,
GOT ANY STYLE
TIPS FOR A GUY WHO
HASN'T DATED IN A WHILE
AND NEEDS A NEW LOOK?
— PHIL
NEW MEXICO

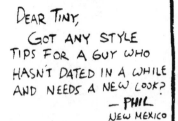

THE SHAGGY

DREADS

SLUGGO

FLAT TOP

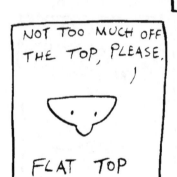

POMPADOUR

'FRO

GOTH

MULLET

EXECUTIVE

MR. PONYTAIL

THE PERM

DEAR T·S·

MY BOYFRIEND BREAKS UP WITH ME AND COMES BACK INTO MY LIFE RIGHT WHEN I THINK I'M OVER HIM. I LOVE HIM BUT I CAN'T KEEP THIS UP. WHAT CAN I DO?

— KEI

YOU'RE LEAVING ME?

DON'T BE LIKE THAT.

IF YOU REALLY LOVE SOMEONE, SET THEM FREE.

IF THEY RETURN, IT WAS MEANT TO BE.

BUT YOU ALWAYS RETURN AND LEAVE ME AGAIN.

AND YOU ALWAYS LET ME RETURN.

'TIL WE MEET AGAIN.

IF YOU LOVE SOMEONE, SET THEM FREE.

IF YOU LOVE YOURSELF, THEN LOCK THE DOOR BEHIND THEM.

DEAR TINY,
HOW SHOULD I
ASK MY GIRLFRIEND
TO MARRY ME?
— DEEZER
S.L.C., UT

I THINK YOU SHOULD CONSIDER HOW <u>NOT</u> TO PROPOSE FIRST.

EEE!
EEE!
EEE!

UH, SORRY... HE URINATES WHEN HE GETS EXCITED SOMETIMES.

① DON'T USE A MONKEY RINGBEARER

I'M SORRY! I'M SORRY!

AMBULANCE

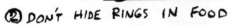

② DON'T HIDE RINGS IN FOOD

PLEASE... LET'S NOT SPOIL THE MOMENT.

③ DON'T PROPOSE AT OVERLY SCENIC LOCATIONS

NO.

HA! BURN!

④ ...OR IN FRONT OF AN AUDIENCE

SO.. YOU'RE GONNA THINK ABOUT IT, RIGHT?... I'LL CALL YOU LATER, OKAY?

⑤ ...ESPECIALLY ON A SECOND DATE.

DEAR TINY,
   MY PARENTS WON'T ACCEPT MY BOYFRIEND BECAUSE OF HIS ETHNICITY. WHAT CAN I DO?

      —KIM
   KIRKLAND, WA

MOM, DAD THIS IS MY NEW BOYFRIEND.

HE'S EVERYTHING YOU WANT.

HE SHARES YOUR HERITAGE

HE BELONGS TO YOUR RELIGION

AND HE WORKS IN YOUR PROFESSION.

WELL, WE'RE IMPRESSED.

I THINK WE'LL GET ALONG WITH HIM BETTER THAN YOUR EX-BOYFRIEND.

WHO SAID WE BROKE UP?

ALMOST DONE HERE, SWEETIE.

COOL.

Dear Tiny,

A friend just revealed his feelings for me. I don't feel the same way, but I do want to keep his friendship. What can I do? —Silver
Santa Monica, CA

I ♡ you.

I'm... flattered.

But it just wouldn't work out.

I don't see you like that at all.

You're like a brother to me.

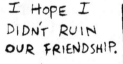

I hope I didn't ruin our friendship.

Oh don't worry, you didn't ruin our friendship.

Good.

...I did.

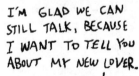

I'm glad we can still talk, because I want to tell you about my new lover.

DEAR TINY,
IS IT WORTH THE RISK OF TELLING A LONGTIME FRIEND HOW I FEEL ABOUT HER?
— LEE
NEW MEXICO

WE'VE BEEN FRIENDS FOR A LONG TIME.

SO I THINK WE COULD MAKE GOOD LOVERS.

WE SHARE THE SAME SENSE OF HUMOR.

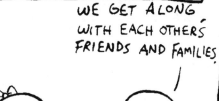
WE GET ALONG WITH EACH OTHER'S FRIENDS AND FAMILIES.

WE SUPPORT EACH OTHER WHEN WE'RE DOWN.

I'M AMAZED THAT WE'VE BEEN "JUST FRIENDS" FOR SO LONG.

YOU DON'T THINK WE'D BE "JUST FRIENDS" FOR SO LONG IF WE FOUND EACH OTHER ATTRACTIVE, DO YOU?

BUT I'VE ALWAYS FOUND YOU ATTRA...
...OH.
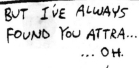

77

DEAR TINY,
I STARTED SEEING THIS GUY AND WITHOUT EXPLANATION HE STOPPED CONTACTING ME AND BEGAN TO AVOID ME. HE WON'T EVEN TELL ME WE'RE THROUGH. WHAT CAN I DO?
— KRYSTAL
ALBUQUERQUE, NM

I LIKE YOU.

BUT I DON'T WANT TO HURT YOU.

SO IT'S BEST IF WE DON'T SEE EACH OTHER EVER AGAIN.

THAT WAY WE BOTH WIN.

WHAT?! HOW DO WE BOTH WIN?

I'M LEFT WITH UNRESOLVED FEELINGS OF REJECTION...

... WHILE YOU PLACE YOURSELF IN A POSITION OF POWER BY PLAYING AVOIDANCE GAMES!

ARE YOU STILL HUNG UP ON THAT? LET IT GO, IT'S ALL IN THE PAST.

DEAR TINY,

I FELL IN LOVE WITH MY FRIEND.
NOW SHE'S ACTING LIKE I'M OBSESSED.
SHE SAYS I SCARED HER OFF, I
DON'T KNOW HOW. IT'S NOT LIKE I
ALWAYS CALL HER, WRITE HER OR GO
TO HER HOUSE, WHAT DO I DO?
— TIM
EVERETT, WA

THEY SAY EXPERIENCE
IS THE BEST TEACHER,
SO HERE'S ONE OF MINE.

THIS IS AN OLD FRIEND   HELLO.
WHO AGREED TO HELP
ME WITH YOUR QUESTION.

SO WHY
DID YOU
PUSH ME
OUT OF
YOUR LIFE?

WELL, I DID
REALLY LIKE
YOU WHEN
WE WERE
FRIENDS.

YOU WERE FUNNY,
KIND, AND YOU
MADE ME FEEL
COMFORTABLE
AROUND YOU.

BUT WHEN YOU
TOLD ME YOU
WANTED TO BE
MORE THAN FRIENDS
I FREAKED.

I WAS SCARED
OF GETTING
INVOLVED WITH
YOU.

I KNEW I'D
JUST HURT YOU
SO I KEPT YOU
AT A DISTANCE.

BUT I WAS
YOUNGER THEN,
AND MAYBE
AVOIDING YOU WAS
IMMATURE OF ME.

SO DO YOU
WANT TO BE
MY FRIEND
AGAIN AND
STOP AVOIDING
ME?

BUT WE GET
ALONG SO
WELL NOW.

DEAR TS

WHY DO MEN TALK ABOUT FREEDOM SO MUCH, BUT END UP GOING OUT WITH WOMEN WHO TIE THEM DOWN?

—FELICIA

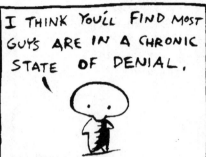

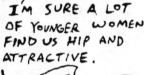

DON'T WORRY, I KNOW EXACTLY WHERE WE ARE!

OF COURSE SHE'LL COME BACK TO ME. SHE LOVES ME.

DEAR TINY,

MY BOYFRIEND DUMPED ME. HE STILL WANTS TO BE BUDDIES AND I DON'T. HOW CAN I GET HIM TO GO AWAY?

—PAULINE
SEATTLE, WA

MAYBE YOU CAN BE THAT FRIEND HE REALLY DOESN'T WANT TO BE AROUND.

I KNOW WE USED TO DATE, BUT WHAT'S YOUR NAME AGAIN?

THE FORGETFUL FRIEND

...SO I NEEDED SOMEONE TO TALK TO. MY LIFE IS SO MESSED UP RIGHT NOW... HEY! ARE YOU THERE? WAKE UP!

ZZZZ

INSENSITIVE FRIEND

WAS I NOT SUPPOSED TO BRING UP YOUR BED WETTING IN FRONT OF PEOPLE?

THE GOSSIPY FRIEND

OOOPS, FORGOT MY CASH. YOU DON'T MIND GETTING THE BILL AGAIN, DO YA?

MOOCHING FRIEND

LET'S SEE... I HAVE A DATE TONIGHT... NEXT WEEK I'M GOING TO SOME GUY'S BEACH HOUSE...

THE BUSY FRIEND

OW!

BONK!

ROCK-THROWING FRIEND

FAKED EVERY ONE.

THE HONEST FRIEND

DEAR TINY,
WHAT SHOULD I GET
MY LOVER FOR
CHRISTMAS?

—VANESSA

TINY SEPU-CLAUSES

HO-HO-HO!

HOLIDAY
GIFTS
FOR
LOVERS

FISHNET X-MAS STOCKINGS

I CAN'T WAIT TO
SEE WHAT FILLS
THAT X-MAS DAY!

A HOT TODDY

TODD

...WITH
A HOT
BODY!

RISQUÉ X-MAS COOKIES

WHAT'S UP WITH
THE THREE-
LEGGED
GINGERBREAD
MAN?

A NUTCRACKER

=CRACK=

YOU ARE
MY DOG!
BEG!

GENETICALLY ALTERED GIANT MISTLETOE

YOU DON'T JUST
'KISS' UNDER
THESE BAD
BOYS, BABY!

THE 'SOULFUL X-MAS' CD

SERIOUSLY, MY
FAVORITE SEASONAL
MAKEOUT ALBUM.

YULE LOG

IT'S SO
MASSIVE!

IS IT SUPPOSED TO
VIBRATE LIKE THAT?

CENSORED

HAPPY HOLIDAYS
WHATEVER YOU
CELEBRATE!

DEAR TINY,
IS IT WISE FOR ME TO PURSUE AN ONLINE RELATIONSHIP WITH SOMEONE I'VE NEVER MET?
—NAIVE? S.L.C. UT

SO... DESCRIBE YOURSELF TO ME.

I'M CHINESE...

I HAVE SHORT HAIR...

I'M SMALL...

I HAVE A SQUARE FACE...

AND I DRESS IN BLACK.

WOW! YOU SOUND GORGEOUS!

THANKS.

DUDE! TELL HIM YOU'RE INTO CHICKS TOO!

DEAR TINY,
I GOT HER A RING,
NOW WHAT?

— JASON

ASKING IS EASY. YOU SHOULD FIGURE OUT WHAT YOU'LL SAY IF SHE SAYS "NO."

HA! I CAN'T BELIEVE YOU FELL FOR THAT! I'D NEVER REALLY ASK YOU.

OH WAIT... I MEANT TO ASK MY OTHER LADY.

WELL, HOW 'BOUT YOUR SISTER? SHE LIKES ME, RIGHT?

I GUESS I'LL HAVE TO SHARE MY SECRET FORTUNE WITH SOMEONE ELSE.

IT'S A GOOD THING I'M REALLY DRUNK.

I WAS ACTUALLY ASKING FOR... UH..."BILL"... YEAH. I'LL TELL HIM YOU SAID NO.

WE CAN STILL SLEEP TOGETHER THOUGH, RIGHT?

DEAR TINY,
MY BOYFRIEND AND I HAVE BEEN DATING FOR A YEAR NOW. HE'S GOING TO LEAVE FOR COLLEGE SOON AND WANTS TO SLEEP WITH ME BEFORE HE GOES. I'M NOT SURE I'M READY YET. WHAT SHOULD I DO?
— CONFUSED

I'M NOT SURE I'M READY. IF YOU LOVE ME YOU WON'T PRESSURE ME. LET'S WAIT A WHILE, OKAY?

BETTER TO WAIT NOW THAN WAIT LATER.

85

DEAR TINY,

MY BOYFRIEND ALWAYS GETS
ME BAD GIFTS AND I'M TOO NICE
TO TELL HIM HE HAS BAD TASTE.
HOW CAN I LET HIM KNOW
WITHOUT HURTING HIM?
— GAYLE
S.F. CA

PERHAPS YOU CAN INFLUENCE
HIS GIFT SELECTION HABITS
BY CHANGING THE GIFTS
YOU GIVE HIM.

OH... A BASKET
FULL OF LITTLE
SOAP BARS... I
DON'T KNOW WHAT
TO SAY.

...A MONITOR
COZY...THE GUYS
AT THE OFFICE
WILL BE JEALOUS.

WELL... I GUESS
YOU CAN NEVER
HAVE TOO MUCH
POTPOURRI...

A DAY AT THE
SPA?...UH, I MEAN,
JUST A DAY?

...AND LET ME GUESS,
ANOTHER BEANIE
BABY... WONDERFUL.

I WAS JUST THINKING
I NEEDED A NEW
BOOK ON DÉCOLLETAGE.

BACK STREET BOYS AND
N'SYNC CDS? YOU
SHOULDN'T HAVE.
I MEAN REALLY.

DEAR TINY,

MY GIRLFRIEND GETS SO JEALOUS OF MY FEMALE FRIENDS THAT I CAN'T HANG OUT WITH THEM WITHOUT A DRAMA. HOW CAN I REASSURE HER THAT I'M FAITHFUL?

— FLUSTERED

LISTEN, I KNOW YOU'RE INSECURE ABOUT ME GOIN' OUT WITH MY FEMALE FRIENDS.

AND I'VE ALWAYS TRIED TO ASSURE YOU THAT I ONLY LOVE YOU.

BUT I CAN'T CONVINCE A PERSON WHO DOESN'T TRUST ME.

YOU'RE PUTTING ME IN AN UNFAIR POSITION.

I'M TIRED OF YOUR CONSTANT ACCUSATIONS AND SUSPICIONS.

I'M SICK OF BEING BLAMED FOR SOMETHING I HAVE NEVER DONE AND WOULD NEVER DO.

SO YOU HAVE TO GROW UP AND BE AN ADULT IF YOU WANT OUR LOVE TO GROW.

OKAY. YOU CAN HAVE FEMALE FRIENDS. NOW LET'S TALK ABOUT HOW MUCH TIME YOU SPEND WITH THE DOG.

WELL, THAT'S COMPLEX.

DEAR TINY,
   MY FRIEND IS MAD AT ME FOR NEVER HAVING A HUMMER. WHAT SHOULD I DO? — INEXPERIENCED S.L.C. UT

LOTS OF PEOPLE GO THROUGH LIFE WITHOUT GETTING A HUMMER.

SURE THEY'RE NICE, BUT HOW PRACTICAL ARE THEY?

THEY REQUIRE A LOT OF MAINTENANCE,

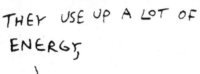

THEY USE UP A LOT OF ENERGY,

AND THEY COST A LOT TOO!

HEY PAL, DO YOU EVEN KNOW WHAT A "HUMMER" IS?

YEAH, THOSE PRICEY ARMY JEEPS.

WHY DO YOU PEOPLE KEEP ASKING HIM QUESTIONS?!

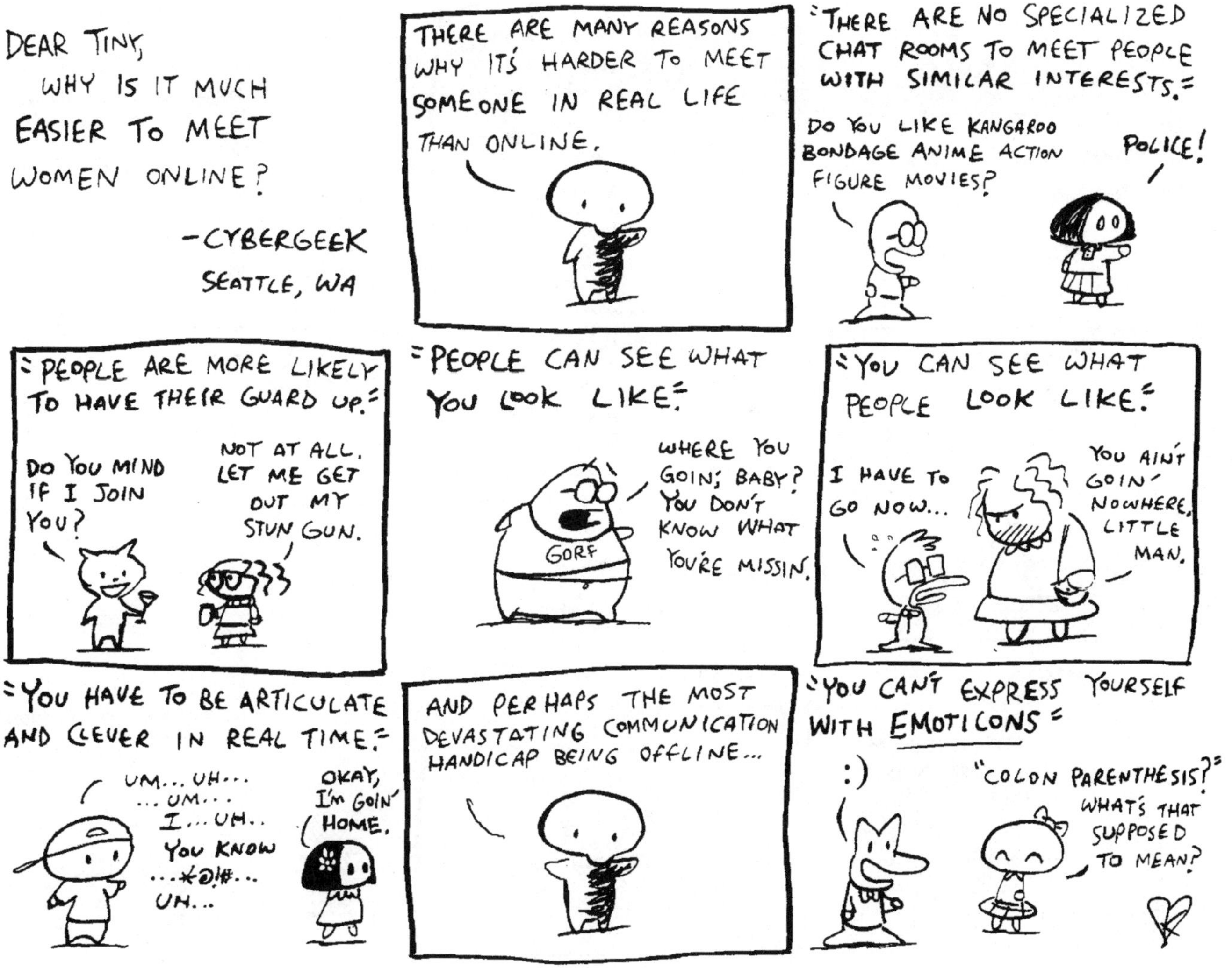

DEAR TINY,
WHY IS IT MUCH EASIER TO MEET WOMEN ONLINE?
-CYBERGEEK
SEATTLE, WA
THERE ARE MANY REASONS WHY IT'S HARDER TO MEET SOMEONE IN REAL LIFE THAN ONLINE.
"THERE ARE NO SPECIALIZED CHAT ROOMS TO MEET PEOPLE WITH SIMILAR INTERESTS."
DO YOU LIKE KANGAROO BONDAGE ANIME ACTION FIGURE MOVIES?
POLICE!
"PEOPLE ARE MORE LIKELY TO HAVE THEIR GUARD UP."
DO YOU MIND IF I JOIN YOU?
NOT AT ALL. LET ME GET OUT MY STUN GUN.
"PEOPLE CAN SEE WHAT YOU LOOK LIKE."
WHERE YOU GOIN' BABY? YOU DON'T KNOW WHAT YOU'RE MISSIN'.
GORF
"YOU CAN SEE WHAT PEOPLE LOOK LIKE."
I HAVE TO GO NOW...
YOU AIN'T GOIN' NOWHERE, LITTLE MAN.
"YOU HAVE TO BE ARTICULATE AND CLEVER IN REAL TIME."
UM... UH... ...UM... I...UH.. YOU KNOW ...*@!#... UH...
OKAY, I'M GOIN' HOME.
AND PERHAPS THE MOST DEVASTATING COMMUNICATION HANDICAP BEING OFFLINE...
"YOU CAN'T EXPRESS YOURSELF WITH EMOTICONS"
:)
"COLON PARENTHESIS?" WHAT'S THAT SUPPOSED TO MEAN?

OH SMALL AND MIGHTY SEPUKU,

How Do I STOP ATTRACTING THE SAME LOSERS INTO MY LIFE TIME AFTER TIME?

—CLAIRE

MAGIC MIGHT WORK. HERE ARE SOME SPELLS YOU CAN CAST TO KEEP LOSERS AT BAY.

SUMMONING

WHAT DO YOU MEAN, YOU'RE NOT ALONE?

¡PAF!

Voo-Doo Dolls

THAT'S A CUTE DOLLY. WHY ARE YOU SEWING ITS MOUFF...? MMF! MMMFF!!

TRANSMOGRIFY

... WELL, MAYBE NOW I CAN WORK THE "KISS ME I'M A PRINCE" ANGLE.

SLEEP

... AND THEN I FOUND THESE REALLY CUTE RED PUMPS...

ZZZ ZZZZ!

LOVE

HI LADIES, MY FRIEND AND I NOTICED YOU WERE ALONE...

ZAP!

WANNA GET MARRIED?

OH BOY! DO I?

DEAR TINY,
I REALLY LIKE THIS MAN WHO WORKS AT A STARBUCKS AND I THINK HE LIKES ME TOO. WHAT CAN I SAY TO MOVE FROM SHORT CONVERSATIONS TO A REAL DATE?
— JESSICA
SEATTLE, WA

"ASKING A SINGLE GUY OUT ON A DATE IS A CLEAR DEMONSTRATION OF HOW MUCH POWER WOMEN HAVE OVER THEM."
DO YOU WAN... YES!!!

"A GOOD FIRST DATE SHOULD BE CASUAL, LIKE GETTING COFFEE. IT'S ALSO A GOOD INDICATOR OF WHAT YOU CAN EXPECT IF YOU CHOOSE TO BE INTIMATE WITH YOUR DATE."

ESPRESSO — "TO THE POINT"
3 MINUTES! A NEW RECORD. — GRRRR...

LATTE — "TYPICAL"
WOW! WAS IT GOOD FOR YOU TOO?
HUH?... OH YEAH... YOU'RE THE (YAWN) KING.

DE-CAF — "CLUELESS"
SURE YOU CAN SLEEP HERE. I'LL GET THE COT.
...SIGH

TEA — "ROMANTIC"
MORNIN' SUNSHINE!
YOU'RE STILL HERE?

HOT CHOCOLATE — "SENSITIVE"
UH...DO YOU ALWAYS CRY WHEN YOU DO THIS?

CHAI — "EXOTIC"
WAIT HERE. I'LL GET THE BEAR COSTUMES AND PUDDING!

DEAR TINY,

MY BOYFRIEND IS ALWAYS COMPARING ME TO OTHER WOMEN. HE'LL SEE A GIRL AT THE MALL AND JUST OGLE HER IN FRONT OF ME, OR HE'LL TELL ME HOW MUCH HE LIKES HER HAIR OR CLOTHES MORE THAN MINE. WHAT CAN I DO? —LISA SEATTLE, WA

WOULD YOU LOOK AT WHAT SHE'S WEARING? MAN THAT'S HOT!

YOU LIKE THAT?

I BET THOSE LEATHER PANTS WOULD LOOK GOOD ON YOU TOO WHEN YOU LOSE A COUPLE POUNDS.

OH?... HOLD ON.

EXCUSE ME MISS!!

W-WHAT ARE YOU DOING?

YES?

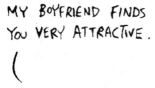

MY BOYFRIEND FINDS YOU VERY ATTRACTIVE.

OH, PLEASE.

SO, WHO ELSE DO YOU THINK IS HOT?

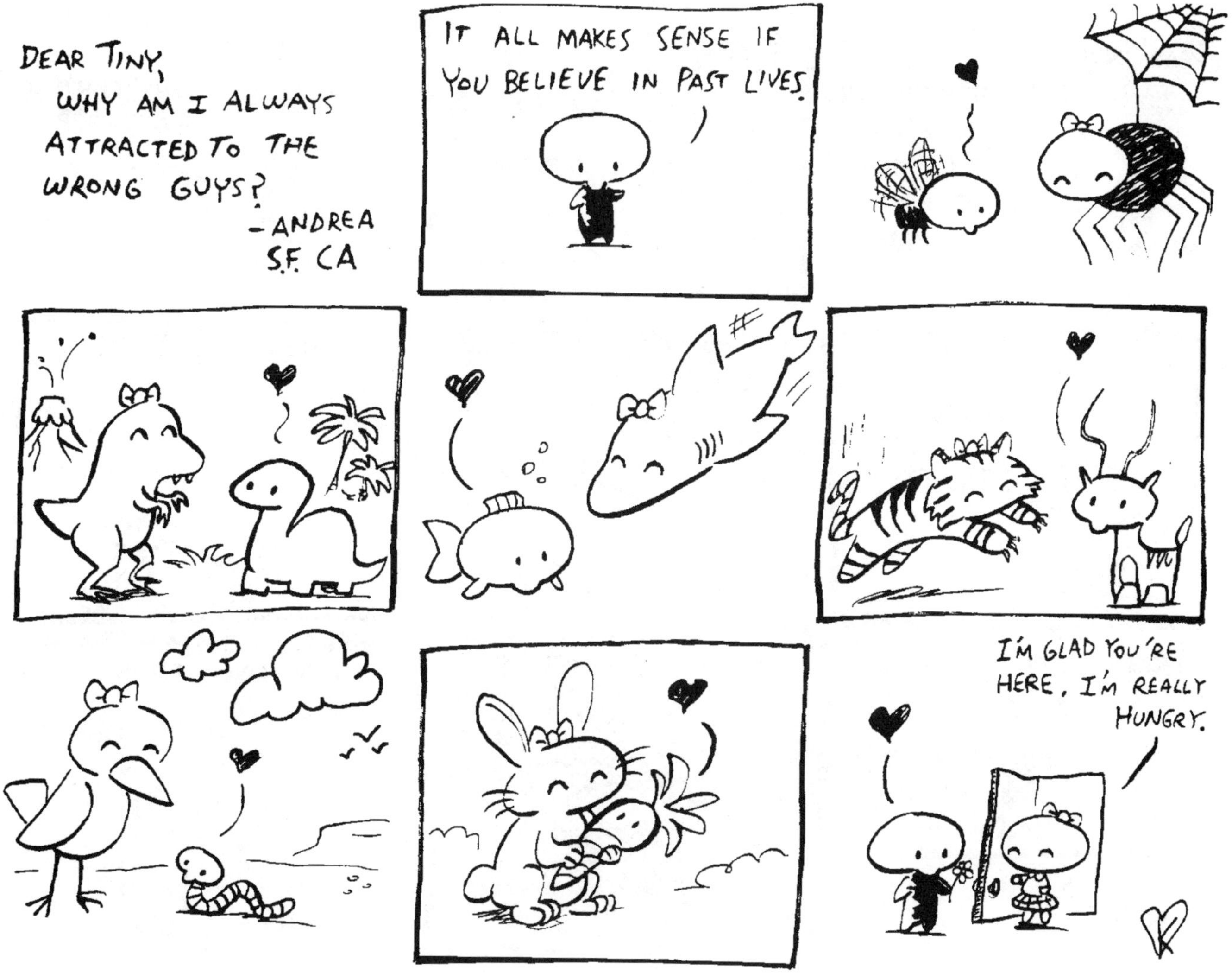
DEAR TINY,
WHY AM I ALWAYS ATTRACTED TO THE WRONG GUYS?
-ANDREA
S.F. CA
IT ALL MAKES SENSE IF YOU BELIEVE IN PAST LIVES.
I'M GLAD YOU'RE HERE. I'M REALLY HUNGRY.

Dear Tiny,

I'm in love with this girl who lives in a different state. How can I keep a relationship growing with her?

— ADAM
SEATTLE, WA

TINY'S TIPS ON MAINTAINING A LONG-DISTANCE ROMANCE.

CONSISTENT EMAILS

WHY CAN'T HE JUST SEND A SIMPLE "HI."

FWD: FUNNY JOKE

SPONTANEOUS GIFTS

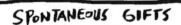

WATER PURIFICATION TABLETS?

OCCASIONAL PHONE CALLS

IT'S 4 A.M.! CAN'T YOU GRASP THE CONCEPT OF TIME ZONES?

WRITE LETTERS

SIGH...

FWD: FUNNY JOKE

TREAT THEM TO A LONG-DISTANCE DATE

OH JOY, A MOVIE PASS AND A McDONALD'S GIFT CERTIFICATE.

SEND FLOWERS

SO DID THEY ARRIVE OKAY?

SURPRISE THEM WITH AN UNANNOUNCED VISIT.

SHE'S STILL IN THE SHOWER.

DEAR TINY,
   I LIKE THIS WOMAN BUT SHE HAS A KID FROM HER PREVIOUS MARRIAGE. I'M SHY ABOUT GETTING TOO CLOSE TO HER BECAUSE OF THAT. WHAT CAN I DO?
— FRANK
SEATTLE, WA

IT MAY SEEM DIFFICULT, BUT THERE ARE MANY BENEFITS TO SEEING SOMEONE WITH KIDS.

DATES ARE MORE FUN

I GOT US ALL WWF TICKETS!   OH.   YAY!

GIFT OPTIONS ARE COOLER

A SONY PLAYSTATION?   HAPPY ANNIVERSARY HON!

DINING OUT IS CHEAPER

SO WHO WANTS PIZZA?   I DO! ME! ME! I DO! ME!   PIZZA AGAIN ... WHAT A SURPRISE.

YOU CAN MENTOR THE KIDS

... AND THAT'S ANOTHER WAY I USED TO CUT CLASS.   COOL! YOU ROCK!

AND LEARN FROM THEM.

... AND THAT'S HOW YOU ALTER YOUR CREDIT ON THE NET.   COOL! YOU KIDS ROCK!

BUT IF YOU JUST WANT TO GET AWAY FROM THE KIDS FOR INTIMATE OCCASIONS, YOU CAN ALWAYS CALL A BABY-SITTER.

THANKS FOR WATCHING THE KIDS WHILE WE WERE OUT. CAN I TAKE YOU HOME?   SURE, WHERE DO YOU LIVE?

DEAR TINY,
WHY IS IT THAT WHEN I FIND MYSELF ATTRACTED TO PEOPLE I FIND THEM NOT VERY INTERESTING. BUT THE PEOPLE I FIND MOST INTERESTING ARE NOT SEXUALLY ATTRACTIVE TO ME? — CORTNIE SEATTLE, WA

THAT'S A COMPLEX QUESTION. I ASKED THE PROFESSOR TO HELP ANSWER IT.

I BROUGHT SLIDES. LIGHTS PLEASE.

IN NATURE OUR PURPOSE IS TO ATTRACT A MATE AND REPRODUCE. THERE ARE MANY WAYS TO ATTRACT THEM.

♪♫ HEY GIRL! YOU'RE FINE! MMM-MM!

BEEP BEEP! ♪ THUMPA THUMPA

EXCUSE ME MISS. CAN I BUY YOU A DRINK?

ONE OF THE MOST POWERFUL WAYS TO ATTRACT A MATE IS WITH PHEROMONES. PEOPLE WITH HIGH AMOUNTS OF THIS CHEMICAL DON'T HAVE TO WORK HARD AT ALL TO ATTRACT A MATE.

:GRUNT: LET'S GO BACK TO MY PLACE.

:GIGGLE: OKAY.

BUT BABY, THIS IS OUR HONEYMOON!

HIGH LEVEL   LOW LEVEL

TO COMPENSATE, THOSE WITH LOW AMOUNTS OF PHEROMONES DEVELOP THEIR PERSONALITIES AS AN ATTEMPT TO ATTRACT MATES.

...AND AFTER LIVING IN EGYPT WITH MAYA ANGELOU, I TAUGHT PHILOSOPHY IN CHILE.

WOW! I FIND YOU REPULSIVE, BUT YOUR INTERESTING STORIES MAKE YOU SEEM LESS HIDEOUS.

THAT IS WHY MOST "INTERESTING" PEOPLE HAVE NO SEX APPEAL.

THAT'S A VERY "INTERESTING" THEORY PROFESSOR.

YEAH? WELL SO IS YOUR COMIC, JERK.

DEAR TINY,
HOW DOES A DEAF
BOY COMMUNICATE
HIS LOVE TO A
HEARING GIRL?
        — MIKE
    PROVO, UT

(I'VE LEARNED A NEW WAY TO COMMUNICATE WITH YOU.)

(IT CAN EXPRESS MORE THAN I EVER COULD USING SIGN LANGUAGE, WRITING, OR TALKING.)

(I'D LIKE US TO TRY THIS NEW METHOD IF YOU ARE UP TO IT.)

IT SOUNDS GREAT! SHOW ME HOW TO DO IT!

SMOOCH!

Dear Tiny,
  My sister just got back with a guy I think is a total jerk. She says he's changed but I don't believe him. What can I do?   — Big Sis
                  Seattle, WA

WE HAD A FIGHT! I'M DONE WITH HIM!

(A FEW DAYS LATER...)

WE TALKED AND I'M TAKING HIM BACK.

(A FEW MONTHS LATER...)

THAT'S IT! IT'S OVER WITH HIM!

(SOME WEEKS LATER...)

I'M GIVING HIM ONE MORE CHANCE.

(SEVERAL MONTHS LATER...)

NEVER AGAIN! HE'S OUT OF MY LIFE FOR GOOD!

(SOON...)

WE'RE GOING TO TRY AGAIN.

I REALLY THINK IT'S GOING TO WORK THIS TIME.

HE'S REALLY CHANGED.

MAYBE, BUT HAVE YOU?

DEAR TINY,
WHAT'S WRONG WITH BEING NICE? WHY DO PEOPLE SAY I'M "TOO NICE" FOR THEM?
— RANDI
S.L.C. UT

WHAT THEY SAY...

You're too nice for me. I don't deserve you.

WHAT THEY MEAN...

How do I tell you you're unattractive without looking shallow?

WHAT THEY SAY...

I don't want to ruin our friendship.

WHAT THEY MEAN...

... BUT I WOULD IF YOU WERE CUTER.

WHAT THEY SAY...

We have our whole lives ahead of us. Let's not get serious.

WHAT THEY MEAN...

I have my whole life ahead of me. See ya, loser!

WHAT THEY SAY...

I'll give you a call sometime.

WHAT THEY MEAN...

I've already forgotten your name.

DEAR TINY,
 I'M ACTUALLY AN EMPEROR BY
BIRTH BUT I'M LIVING IN EVERETT.
HOW DO I CONVINCE MY FRIENDS
OF MY REGAL DESCENT?

                EMPEROR STU
              — EVERETT, WA

THERE ARE A VARIETY
OF COST-EFFECTIVE WAYS
TO LET THE MASSES KNOW
WHO'S IN CHARGE.

T-SHIRTS

I'M WITH
PEASANT

BUMPER STICKERS

HONK IF
YOU'RE MY
SUBJECT

DON'T BLAME
ME, I VOTED
AUTHORITARIAN

CUSTOMIZED CAP

MY OTHER
HAT IS A
CROWN!

VANITY PLATES

BOW 2 ME
NOV   USA   01

PERSONALIZED MUG

#1
EMPEROR

BUSINESS CARDS

JOE
CITIZEN
EMPEROR
LOW RATES! IRON FIST!

WEB SITE

EMPEROR CAM!
SEE ME IN MY
"NEW CLOTHES"
$3.95/MONTH

DEAR TINY,
I JUST READ THAT SCIENTISTS ARE NOW ABLE TO FERTILIZE EGGS WITHOUT USING SPERM. ARE MEN BECOMING OBSOLETE?
— SOYLENT BOB

I'VE ASKED THIS CULTURAL ANALYST WHAT HER TAKE ON IT IS.

SO, DO YOU THINK MEN ARE BECOMING IRRELEVANT IN TODAY'S SOCIETY?

OF COURSE NOT. THAT'S A PARANOID FANTASY. NOT ALL MEN WILL BE IRRELEVANT.

ONLY THE INSECURE, POSSESSIVE ONES...

...THAT ARE SELF-OBSESSED AND REFUSE TO GROW UP

ESPECIALLY WHEN COMMITTING TO AN ADULT RELATIONSHIP.

I THINK YOU KNOW THE TYPE.

I KNEW WE SHOULD'VE BROKEN UP AFTER THE STRIP.

NOW LET'S TALK ABOUT THE RELEVANCE OF ADVICE COMIC STRIPS.

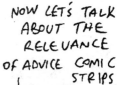  

DEAR TINY,
AFTER GOING FROM RELATIONSHIP
TO RELATIONSHIP AND NOT SEEMING
TO "GET IT RIGHT," WHAT MAKES
US KEEP GOING? IS THERE
SOMETHING IN LOVE WORTH
OBTAINING?
                    —LUKE
                    S.F., CA

LOVE IS WORTH IT FOR ALL THE "SUPER POWERS" YOU GET IN A RELATIONSHIP.

INVISIBILITY

HONEY, I NEED YOUR HELP IN THE KITCHEN. HON? HELLO?

ASTRAL TRAVEL

...SO IT'S FOURTH DOWN 10 SECONDS TO GO...

TELEPATHY

I SENSE THAT YOU'RE UPSET.

HEIGHTENED AWARENESS

MMMM

SUPERMEMORY

I CAN'T BELIEVE YOU FORGOT WE ATE CHINESE FOR OUR FIRST DATE.

REALLY? I THOUGHT YOU HATE CHINESE FOOD.

SPEED

I THINK WE SHOULD CONSIDER MARRI...

ZIP!

TIME MANIPULATION

ARE YOU READY YET? WE'RE GONNA MISS THE MOVIE!

RELAX! WE'LL MAKE IT!

Dear T.S.,
HELP! WHY DON'T WOMEN FIND ME ATTRACTIVE?

—DESPERATE, BUT NOT SERIOUS
S.L.C., UT

CELEBRITIES SEEM TO HAVE NO TROUBLE ATTRACTING PEOPLE...

AND WITH "REALITY ENTERTAINMENT" EVERYONE HAS AN OPPOTUNITY TO BECOME A STAR. TRY THESE WAYS TO GRAB YOUR 15 MINUTES.

"BREAK A RECORD"

I INTEND TO EAT 500 CANS OF CHILI IN 5 HOURS.

"MARKET `EXTREME` HOME VIDEOS OF YOURSELF"

EXTREME!!!
FREE STYLE WALKING!!
WATCH HIM GO DOWN AN UP ESCALATOR!

"BE A GAME SHOW CONTESTANT"

I SHOULDN'T HAVE USED ALL MY LIFELINES ON THE FIRST QUESTION.

A. HIROSHIGE   C. SINCIPUT
B. ATRAHASIS   D. PANCHA SILA

"PUT UP A WEB PAGE"

HEY. CHECK OUT THIS LOSER.

AW...THAT HAS TO BE FAKE. NO ONE IS THAT LAME.

"BE A TALK SHOW GUEST"

TODAY: "SURPRISE SEX CHANGE OPERATIONS"

"COMPETE IN THE ULTIMATE FIGHTING CHAMPIONSHIPS"

EXTRA!!!
MAN DIES IN CAGE MATCH!

DEAR TINY,

DOES HEARING ABOUT OTHER PEOPLE'S LOVE LIVES EVER MAKE YOU CYNICAL ABOUT YOUR OWN?

— MELISSA
S.L.C. UT

KINDERGARTEN

 DO YOU WANT TO PLAY WITH ME?

 GO AWAY, STINKY PANTS!

ELEMENTARY SCHOOL

 I MADE YOU A VALENTINE'S DAY CARD.

 EEEW! IT'S GOT SEPU-COOTIES ON IT! YUCK!

JR. HIGH

 UH... HELLO? YOU DON'T KNOW ME BUT I'M IN YOUR HISTORY CLASS AND I... WHAT?... NO, I'M THE ONE IN THE BACK WITH GLASSES... HELLO? ...HELLO?

HIGH SCHOOL

 WE CAN GO OUT AS LONG AS WE PRETEND NOT TO KNOW EACH OTHER IN PUBLIC.

COLLEGE

  I'D LOVE TO GO OUT. WHAT FRAT DO YOU BELONG TO?

FIRST LOVE

 I'D LOVE TO MARRY YOU, BUT THE GUY I'VE BEEN SEEING BEHIND YOUR BACK MIGHT GET HURT.

LAST LOVE

 I INVITED THIS CUTE GUY I JUST MET IN LINE TO SEE THE MOVIE WITH US, THEN I'M GOIN' HOME WITH HIM AFTER. 'SUP.

 NO... "OTHER PEOPLE'S LOVE LIVES DON'T MAKE ME CYNICAL ABOUT MY OWN AT ALL."

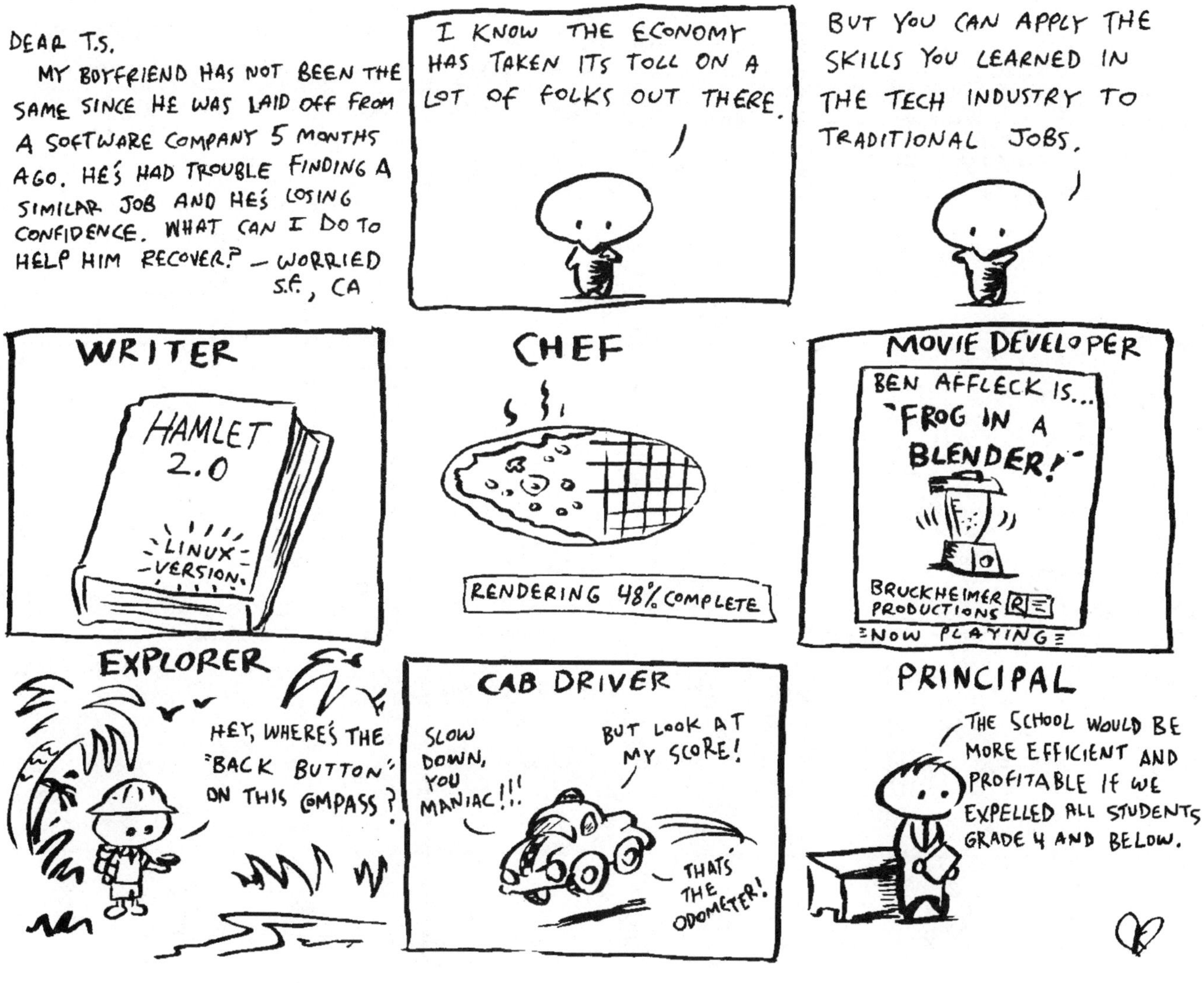
DEAR T.S.
MY BOYFRIEND HAS NOT BEEN THE SAME SINCE HE WAS LAID OFF FROM A SOFTWARE COMPANY 5 MONTHS AGO. HE'S HAD TROUBLE FINDING A SIMILAR JOB AND HE'S LOSING CONFIDENCE. WHAT CAN I DO TO HELP HIM RECOVER? —WORRIED S.F., CA
I KNOW THE ECONOMY HAS TAKEN ITS TOLL ON A LOT OF FOLKS OUT THERE.
BUT YOU CAN APPLY THE SKILLS YOU LEARNED IN THE TECH INDUSTRY TO TRADITIONAL JOBS.
WRITER
HAMLET 2.0
LINUX VERSION
CHEF
RENDERING 48% COMPLETE
MOVIE DEVELOPER
BEN AFFLECK IS... "FROG IN A BLENDER!"
BRUCKHEIMER PRODUCTIONS
R
NOW PLAYING
EXPLORER
HEY, WHERE'S THE "BACK BUTTON" ON THIS COMPASS?
CAB DRIVER
SLOW DOWN, YOU MANIAC!!!
BUT LOOK AT MY SCORE!
THATS THE ODOMETER!
PRINCIPAL
THE SCHOOL WOULD BE MORE EFFICIENT AND PROFITABLE IF WE EXPELLED ALL STUDENTS GRADE 4 AND BELOW.

DEAR TINY,

IT SEEMS LIKE ANYTIME I TALK TO MEN THEY ALWAYS THINK I'm FLIRTING WITH THEM. HOW DO I STOP GIVING OFF THE WRONG SIGNALS?

— GRACE
S.F. CA

COMMUNICATION BETWEEN MEN AND WOMEN HAS NEVER BEEN VERY CLEAR.

THIS IS DUE TO A KIND OF AURAL DYSLEXIA, COMMON IN MOST PEOPLE.

YOU MAY SAY:

UH... I THINK THEY JUST ASKED FOR YOUR NUMBER.

NOW SERVING 6

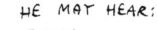

HE MAY HEAR:

UH... I THINK YOU SHOULD ASK FOR MY NUMBER.

NOW SERVING 6

OR YOU MAY SAY:

SORRY, I HAVE A BOYFRIEND.

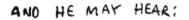

AND HE MAY HEAR:

I HAVE A SORRY BOYFRIEND.

AND THE MISCOMMUNICATION SEEMS TO GET WORSE ONCE YOU'RE INVOLVED IN A RELATIONSHIP.

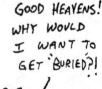

DO YOU EVER THINK ABOUT GETTING "MARRIED"?

GOOD HEAVENS! WHY WOULD I WANT TO GET "BURIED"?!

DEAR TINY,
WHY IS IT THAT GUYS PLAY FEMALE CHARACTERS ON VIDEO GAMES? I'M NOT COMPLAINING, JUST CURIOUS.
—EVE
S.F., CA

I ASKED MY NEPHEW TO HELP EXPLAIN THIS CULTURAL PHENOMENON.

SUP.

SO WHY DO YOU CHOOSE FEMALE CHARACTERS IN VIDEO GAMES?

ARE YOU KIDDING? GIRLS ROCK!

MICHELLE YEOH TOTALLY KICKED IN "CROUCHING TIGER"!

BUFFY AND DARK ANGEL ARE THE BEST SHOWS ON T.V.!

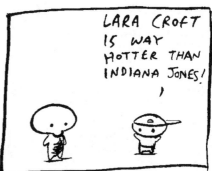

LARA CROFT IS WAY HOTTER THAN INDIANA JONES!

I LOVE THE POWER PUFF GIRLS!

AND CHYNA IS MY FAVORITE WRESTLER!

SO... DO YOU HAVE ANY MALE ROLE MODELS AT ALL?

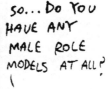

PIKACHU! PIKACHU!

DEAR TINY,
   WHAT DO YOU DO IF YOU'RE ATTRACTED TO SOMEONE A LOT YOUNGER THAN YOU? WHAT IS IT ABOUT YOUTH THAT IS SO INTOXICATING? (I'M NOT SICK, JUST WONDERING.)
                              —FELICIA
                              SEATTLE, WA

I SUPPOSE ON THE SURFACE "MAY-DECEMBER" RELATIONSHIPS SEEM EXCITING AND FUN.

BUT YOU MAY WANT TO CONSIDER SOME POSSIBLE PROBLEMS TO A NABOKOVIAN LOVE AFFAIR.

CONFLICTING PRIORITIES

WE'RE LATE FOR MY FIRM'S PARTY, HON.

CAN'T YOU SEE I'M BUSY, BABE?!

BEEP BOOP ZIP

CULTURAL BARRIERS

LISTENING TO "THE POLICE", DARLING? I LOVED THAT BAND AT YOUR AGE.

"HEL-LO", LIKE THIS AN OLD "PUFF DADDY" TRACK, NOT SOME OLD HIPPIE BAND, "DUH"!

EMOTIONAL EXTORTION

GIMME SOME MONEY OR I'M LEAVING.

ANYTHING YOU WANT MY LAST CHANCE AT "HAPPINESS".

CHEMICAL DEPENDENCY

I NEED SOME PAXIL, VIAGRA, ROGAINE, RETIN-A, LEPTIN, CONTACT LENS SOLUTION, AND GRECIAN FORMULA.

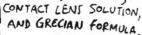

PHARMACY

OF COURSE OUTER BEAUTY IS NOT THE ONLY THING THAT MAKES YOUTH ATTRACTIVE. WHAT COUNTS IS ON THE "INSIDE."

YOU'RE GOING TO NEED A KIDNEY FOR YOUR TRANSPLANT.

GOT ONE, DOC.

HEY! YOU SAID THAT FORM WAS FOR MY CAR LOAN!

108

DEAR TINY,

WHAT CAN YOU DO ABOUT SOMEONE WHO HAS A CRUSH ON A REPUBLICAN? CAN A RELATIONSHIP BETWEEN A LIBERAL DEMOCRAT AND A CONSERVATIVE SURVIVE?

— CAROLINA S.F. CA

A BIPARTISAN RELATIONSHIP HAS AS MUCH CHANCE OF WORKING AS ANY OTHER KIND, WITH A FEW MORE DISAGREEMENTS ON KEY ISSUES.

DINING OUT

TWO FOR SMOKING OR NON?

NON SMOKING!

SMOKING!

T.V.

X-FILES!

TOUCHED BY AN ANGEL!

OUTINGS

THIS IS A NICE PLACE.

...FOR A MALL.

MOVIES

LET'S SEE THIS SEXY NC-17 FILM.

GROSS! I WANT TO SEE THIS BLOODY PG-13 SHOOT 'EM UP!

MUSIC

I GOT THE NEW DIXIE CHICKS CD.

YOU KNOW I FIND THEIR LYRICS TOO RISQUÉ.

BUT DESPITE THESE PETTY DIFFERENCES, CONCESSIONS CAN BE MADE TO SUSTAIN A WORKING RELATIONSHIP.

THAT WAS GREAT! DO YOU HAVE A SMOKE?

PERHAPS I NEED TO RETHINK MY POSITION ON ABSTINENCE.

DEAR TINY,
HOW DO YOU KNOW WHEN
YOU'VE MET YOUR SOUL MATE?

— MICHELLE
SEATTLE, WA

WELL, IF YOU BELIEVE IN
THE IDEA OF A "SOUL MATE"
THEN YOU SHOULD BELIEVE
YOU'RE PREDESTINED TO MEET
THEM NO MATTER WHAT.

HOWEVER, UNTIL THAT TIME
YOU'LL HAVE TO DEAL WITH
OTHER TYPES OF COSMIC
"SOUL ASSOCIATES".

THE SOUL JERK

THANKS FOR THE CHOCOLATES, HON.

THEY'RE LOW-FAT. YOU COULD USE IT.

THE SOUL PLAYA

OH... HI BABY. I DIDN'T EXPECT YOU TO BE HOME SO EARLY.

THE SOUL CREEP

I GOT YOU A PRESENT FOR OUR ANNIVERSARY.

WE BROKE UP FIVE YEARS AGO!!!

THE SOUL NEANDERTHAL

I BET YOU CAN'T WAIT TO GET OUT OF COLLEGE AND HAVE A REAL MAN TAKE CARE OF YOU.

THE SOUL THIEF

YOU SOLD MY CAR?!..

IT WASN'T A GIFT TO ME?

THE SOUL FLAKE

OUR WEDDING WAS YESTERDAY? I THOUGHT IT WAS NEXT WEEK.

DEAR TINY,

I HAVE AN AMAZING GIRLFRIEND. HOW DO I KEEP HER THINKING I'M AMAZING TOO?

—TOR
SEATTLE, WA

TINY'S TIPS TO AMAZE YOUR LOVER!

BECAUSE THOSE WHO CAN'T DO, TEACH.

SERENADE THEM

I DID IT ALL FOR THA NOOKIE!

-??

TAKE THEM DANCING

WHERE YA GOIN'? I DIDN'T BUY YOU A LAP DANCE YET!

SURPRISE THEM WITH A TRIP

GOOD NEWS! I GOT US TWO BUS TICKETS TO OMAHA! OMAHA BABY!!!

RECITE A POEM

I WROTE THIS FOR YOU. I CALL IT "TAKE IT OFF AND SHAKE IT".

GET THEM A GIFT

A CAN OF SOUP?

YOU CAN THANK ME TONIGHT, TOOTS!

PREPARE AN EXOTIC MEAL

IT'S PANDA!

UMPH!!

LEARN A MAGIC TRICK

HON?... YOU OKAY? ...UH-OH.

DEAR TINY,

MY FRIEND RECENTLY GOT ME A GIFT FROM VICTORIA'S SECRET, YET UPON OPENING IT I DISCOVERED SCENTED LAUNDRY DETERGENT AND DRYER SHEETS. SHOULD I HIT HIM?
— LINZ
EVERETT, WA

SURPRISE!!!

I HOPE YOU LIKE IT!

IT'S FROM VICTORIA'S SECRET!

OH WOW! I LOVE THEIR STUFF! THANKS!

RIP! TEAR! RIP!

???

HA! YOU FELL FOR IT!

I TRICKED YOU! MAN THAT WAS FUNNY!

YEAH, THAT WAS PRETTY FUNNY. THANK YOU HUG?

SURE.

... AND THAT'S WHEN SHE KNEED ME AND I BLACKED OUT, DOC.

NOW THAT'S A FUNNY TRICK.

DEAR TINY,
THIS IS FROM A FRIEND — IF ONE'S
SPOUSE IS NO LONGER INTERESTED IN
SEX THOUGH THEY ARE MARRIED TO
A BOMBSHELL, DOES IT MEAN THE
BOMBSHELL SHOULDN'T FEEL GUILTY
FOR SEEKING AFFECTION ELSEWHERE?
—ANON.
KC., MO

THAT'S A VERY GOOD QUESTION. MY ADVI...

HOLD ON A SEC CHIEF!

HUH?

WHY DON'T YOU LET ME FIELD THIS QUESTION?

COME AGAIN?

YOU'RE ALWAYS ANSWERING QUESTIONS AND I THINK YOU DESERVE A BREAK.

WHAT KIND OF FRIEND WOULD I BE IF I DIDN'T RELIEVE YOUR BURDEN ONCE IN A WHILE?

WELL... OKAY, WHY NOT. GIVE IT A SHOT.

COOL! YOU WON'T REGRET IT!

AHEM. I THINK YOUR BOMBSHELL FRIEND SHOULDN'T FEEL GUILTY AT ALL.

!!!

IN FACT, I'M AVAILABLE RIGHT NOW IF SHE WANTS TO G-UMF!!!

OKAY, THAT'S ENOUGH! THANKS FOR THE HELP!

113

OH GREAT TINY ONE,
THERE IS GUY A AND GUY B. GUY A
IS NEAR, VERY HOT, KIND AND SUPPORTIVE.
I'M VERY INTERESTED IN HIM. GUY
B IS FAR AWAY, CUTE, SWEET, BUT
YOUNG. HE SAYS HE'S IN LOVE WITH
ME BUT I'M NOT INTERESTED. WHAT
SHOULD I DO?
— MOLLY
WASHINGTON D.C.

IT SEEMS LIKE YOU'VE ALREADY MADE UP YOUR MIND ON WHAT YOU WANT TO DO.

SO I GUESS THE ONLY THING YOU SHOULD DO IS TO BREAK THE NEWS TO GUY B IN A WAY THAT SOFTENS THE BLOW. GIFTS SOMETIMES HELP THEM TO FORGET THE PAIN.

MEN'S MAG SUBSCRIPTION

I'M SURE TO FIND A NEW LADY WITH ALL THIS FOOL PROOF ADVICE!!!

MUSHROOM GIFT BASKET

SORRY TO HEAR IT DIDN'T WORK OUT WITH YOU TWO.

DUDE! HOW DO YOU GET YOUR VOICE TO ECHO LIKE THAT?

A PET

SHE TORE UP YOUR HEART AND I'LL TEAR UP YOUR FURNITURE.

CLOWN-O-GRAM

HYUK!

HYUK!

HONK!

AMNESIA PILLS

DID I JUST TAKE THESE?

HAVE YOUR NYMPHOMANIAC FRIEND TELL HIM

SORRY YOU HAD TO LEARN ABOUT IT FROM ME. WANNA GO TO BED?

BEST BREAKUP EVER!!!

'PUKU—
WHY IS IT THAT THE
GIRLS I HAVE MOST IN
COMMON WITH ARE THE ONES
WHO WANT NOTHING TO DO
WITH ME?
—SQUINTY

TWO WORDS, BABY,
"OPPOSITES ATTRACT."

SO JUST BE THE
OPPOSITE OF THE
TYPE OF PERSON YOU
WANT TO BE WITH.

"IF YOU WANT SOMEONE
KIND, BE MEAN"

WHAT DO YOU
WANT, LOSER?

I WAS THINKIN'
ABOUT YOU AND
GOT YOU A
GIFT,
SWEETIE.

"IF YOU WANT SOMEONE
SEXY, BE WHOLESOME"

I FIND AMISH
MEN REALLY
HOT!

I FEEL A BARN
RAISING COMIN'
ON.

"IF YOU WANT SOMEONE
SMART, BE DUMB"

POOR THING.
LET ME TIE
YOUR SHOES
FOR YOU.

UH...DAW!
TANKS PRETTY
LADY! DUH!

"IF YOU WANT SOMEONE
RICH, BE POOR"

HAND OVER
YOUR MONEY!

SURE,
GORGEOUS!

"IF YOU WANT SOMEONE
FUNNY, BE DEPRESSED...
OR A POET"

IF THAT DIDN'T
CHEER YOU UP,
HERE'S ANOTHER
JOKE!

HOW CAN YOU
LAUGH WHEN
LIFE IS SO
BLEAK?

"IF YOU WANT SOMEONE
LOYAL, BE DISLOYAL"

I KNOW YOU
DON'T LOVE HER
SO I FORGIVE
YOU.

COOL!

SHE
YOUR
WIFE?

DEAR TINY,
   HOW DO I GET AN EX-GIRLFRIEND BACK TO GIRLFRIEND STATUS?
            —RICH
       SEATTLE, WA

HERE'S A LIST OF METHODS I'VE USED TO TRY AND RECONCILE WITH OLD FLAMES.

HYPNOSIS

I...WAS...WRONG ...TO...LEAVE ...YOU.

BRIBERY

I'M STRANGELY ATTRACTED TO YOU AGAIN.

CLONING

WELL, TECHNICALLY YOU ARE MY GIRLFRIEND AGAIN.

DISGUISES

WE GET ALONG SO WELL, LIKE WE'VE KNOWN EACH OTHER BEFORE.

SI.

ADVERTISE

GOT TINY?

TIME TRAVEL

DUDE! WHO ARE YOU?

I'M THE "FUTURE" YOU HERE TO TELL YOU NOT TO BE SUCH A JERK TO YOUR GIRL ...ALSO, GET A HAIRCUT!

CHANGE YOUR DEFINITION OF "GIRLFRIEND"

I NEVER WANT TO SEE YOU AGAIN!

SO YOU WANT THIS TO BE A LONG-DISTANCE RELATIONSHIP.

DEAR TINY,

Do STRAIGHT MEN GET OFFENDED OR SCARED WHEN GAY MEN COMPLIMENT THEM?

—ANAM
WEST JORDAN, UT

FOR THE MOST PART, STRAIGHT GUYS ARE SECURE ENOUGH WITH THEIR SEXUAL IDENTITY TO BE COOL WITH COMPLIMENTS GIVEN TO THEM BY GAY FOLKS.

HOWEVER, THERE ARE A FEW IRRATIONAL FELLAS WHO CONSIDER SUCH COMMENTS AS INSULTS TO THEIR FRAGILE MASCULINITY.

BUT IN GENERAL, MOST STRAIGHTS ARE LEVELHEADED AND WON'T FREAK OUT BECAUSE SOME GUY FLATTERS THEM.

ALTHOUGH... THERE COULD BE CERTAIN OCCASIONS WHERE EVEN SECURE STRAIGHT GUYS MAY NOT KNOW HOW TO HANDLE A COMPLIMENT FROM A GAY PERSON.

YOU WERE FANTASTIC LAST NIGHT.

UH... COULD WE NOT TALK ABOUT THAT RIGHT NOW?

DEAR TINY,
I'VE BEEN DIGGIN' THIS GIRL FOR THE PAST TWO YEARS BUT WHEN I TRY TO TAKE A STEP BEYOND FRIENDSHIP SHE USES THE "BUSY STUDYING" EXCUSE. AM I GOING NOWHERE FAST?
— MIKE LA, CA

YOU SHOULD OFFER TO STUDY WITH HER AND THEN MAKE YOUR MOVE.

I'M SORRY, BUT I CAN'T STUDY BY CANDLELIGHT AND SOFT MUSIC.

MAYBE A MARTINI WILL HELP.

WHAT DID YOU NEED MY HELP STUDYING?

THE KAMA SUTRA.

YOU KNOW, MASSAGES ARE A CURE FOR WRITER'S BLOCK. LIE DOWN, I'LL SHOW YOU.

COULD YOU HELP ME WITH MY EXPERIMENTS ON PHYSIOLOGICAL RESPONSES TO ORAL STIMULATION?

COME ON, I STUDY ALL THE TIME IN BED. I'M SURE YOU'LL LEARN SOMETHING IF YOU CLIMB IN.

OOPS! I SPILLED THE PHEROMONES I WAS RESEARCHING. HOPE YOU CAN CONTROL YOURSELF.

"SNIFF" "SNIFF"

WHERE YOU GOIN', BABY? I ALWAYS STUDY NAKED.

DEAR TINY,
HOW COME WHEN A WOMAN IS "NEEDY" MEN SWARM LIKE SHARKS, BUT AN INDEPENDENT WOMAN GETS THE SHORT END OF THE STICK?
— LEX

HELP! HELP ME!

MY HERO!

I'VE COME TO RESCUE YOU, FAIR DAMSEL.

HEY, WHAT ARE YOU DOING WITH HER? YOU'RE S'POSED TO BE MY PRINCE CHARMING.

WELL, I FIGURED YOU DIDN'T NEED ME SINCE YOU FREED YOURSELF FROM THE OGRE AND DEFEATED HIS GIANT DRAGON BEFORE I UNSHEATHED MY SWORD.

IF YOU USURP MY TRADITIONAL ROLE IN THE RELATIONSHIP, HOW CAN I EVER BE SECURE WITH MY IDENTITY?

SO YOUR FRAGILE EGO WAS THREATENED BECAUSE YOU COULDN'T PLAY HERO? WELL GUESS WHAT, YOU ONLY PLAY "HERO" BECAUSE WE PLAY "DAMSEL IN DISTRESS" SO WELL.

PLAYING "NEEDY" IS THE OLDEST WAY TO GET YOUR ATTENTION. IN FACT THAT PRINCESS THERE ISN'T EVEN TIED TO THE POLE!

SO YOU GUYS FAKE NEEDING MY HELP?

THAT'S NOT THE ONLY THING WE'RE GOOD AT FAKING, HONEY.

DEAR TINY
HOW CAN I TELL IF MY
COWORKER ADORES ME OR
IS JUST PLAYING OFFICE
POLITICS MINDGAMES?
— ERIC
SF, CA

IT'S HARD TO TELL IF SOMEONE'S HEART IS FOR YOU OR FOR THEIR CAREER.

ONE WAY TO KNOW IS IF THEY USE "BUZZWORDS" TO COMMUNICATE THEIR EMOTIONS.

I THINK WE SHOULD STAY BROKEN UP.

BUT WE'RE BACKWARD COMPATIBLE.

I FELT I NEEDED SOME HORIZONTAL DIVERSIFICATION.

I'VE DECIDED TO OUTSOURCE SOME OF YOUR BEDROOM DUTIES.

WE SHOULD LIMIT OUR AFFAIR TO NONPERSONAL COMMUNICATION CHANNELS.

COOL! MEET YOU IN THE COPY ROOM IN FIVE MINUTES!

I'M NOT CHEATING ON YOU, BABE. I'M PARALLEL PATHING.

YOU KNOW HE STUFFS SOCKS DOWN HIS PANTS TO INFLATE HIS MARKET VALUE.

HIS PRODUCT DID SEEM LESS ROBUST THAN WHAT THE PACKAGE PROMISED.

TINY,
FOR JOB REASONS I MOVED
FAR AWAY FROM MY BOY-
FRIEND. NOW I'M NOT SURE
IF THE RELATIONSHIP CAN
WORK. DOES DISTANCE MAKE
THE HEART GROW FONDER?

DEAR TINY,
I'M 20 AND THE GIRL I LIKE IS 4 YEARS YOUNGER THAN ME. IS IT OKAY TO DATE HER?

— LUKE OHIO

I GUESS IF YOU TWO LIKE EACH OTHER AND HER FOLKS ARE COOL WITH IT, THERE SHOULDN'T BE A PROBLEM. SO MAKE SURE YOU GET THEIR APPROVAL.

SHOW THEM YOU HAVE GOALS

I'M STUDYING TO BE A LAWYER.

I SEE YOU SKIPPED THE LECTURE ON "AGE OF CONSENT" LAWS.

PROVE YOU'RE TRUSTWORTHY

LET'S GO, I TOLD YOUR FOLKS I'D GET YOU HOME BY TEN.

WHY DO YOU CARE? ARE YOU TRYING TO SCORE WITH THEM?

COMPLIMENT THEIR DAUGHTER

YOUR DAUGHTER IS A GREAT KISSER.

MA, GET ME THE BAT.

ALREADY GOT IT FOR YA.

HELP AROUND THE HOUSE

THANKS FOR DINNER. LET ME DO THE DISHES.

SON, THAT'S THE ONLY THING IN THIS HOUSE I'LL LET YOU "DO."

PARTICIPATE IN THEIR HOBBIES

YOUR DAD IS TAKING ME HUNTING WITH HIM.

I HOPE YOU DON'T ACCIDENTALLY GET SHOT LIKE MY LAST BOYFRIEND HE TOOK.

OF COURSE, ONCE YOU WIN OVER THE PARENTS YOU MAY LOSE A GIRLFRIEND.

SO WHY ARE YOU BREAKING UP WITH ME?

I DON'T KNOW... IT JUST FEELS WEIRD TO DATE MY PARENTS' FRIEND.

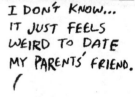

DEAR TINY,
THE GUY I'M SECRETLY IN LOVE
WITH IS MOVING! I'M TOO SCARED
TO TELL HIM HOW I FEEL. DO
YOU HAVE ANY ALTERNATIVES?
— DIANA

THERE ARE MANY WAYS OF
TELLING PEOPLE HOW YOU
FEEL WITHOUT BEING DIRECT.

PUPPETS

PLAYFUL TEASING

TELL ALL HIS FRIENDS HOW YOU FEEL ABOUT HIM...

...THEN TELL HIM YOU HEARD HE LIKES YOU

TELL HIM IN A DIFFERENT LANGUAGE

CONVEY YOUR FEELINGS IN POETRY FORM

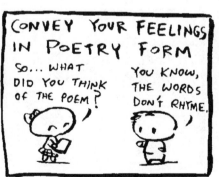

HAVE SOMEONE DRESS LIKE YOU AND TELL HIM

DEAR TINY,
WHY DON'T CHICKS
DIG COMICS?

-CHRIS
S.F., CA

LOOK AT THE
NEW COMIC BOOK
I BOUGHT!

WHY DO YOU SPEND
MONEY ON STUFF
LIKE THAT?

THE STORIES
ARE SO
PREDICTABLE.

THE CHARACTERS
ARE FLAT AND
UNDEVELOPED.

NOT TO MENTION HOW
INSULTING AND OFFENSIVE
THE ARTWORK IS WITH
ITS SEXIST IMAGES
AND GRAPHIC
VIOLENCE.

YOU SHOULD BE READING
BOOKS WITHOUT PICTURES
IN THEM. SOMETHING THAT
WILL EXPAND
YOUR MIND.

YOU MEAN LIKE THOSE
EROTIC THRILLERS WITH
THE BARE-CHESTED DUDE
ON THE COVERS THAT
YOU READ?

HEY, IF THAT'S WHAT IT
TAKES TO STOP YOU FROM
BUGGING ME TO DRESS UP
LIKE "CAT WOMAN" ALL
THE TIME, THEN YEAH!

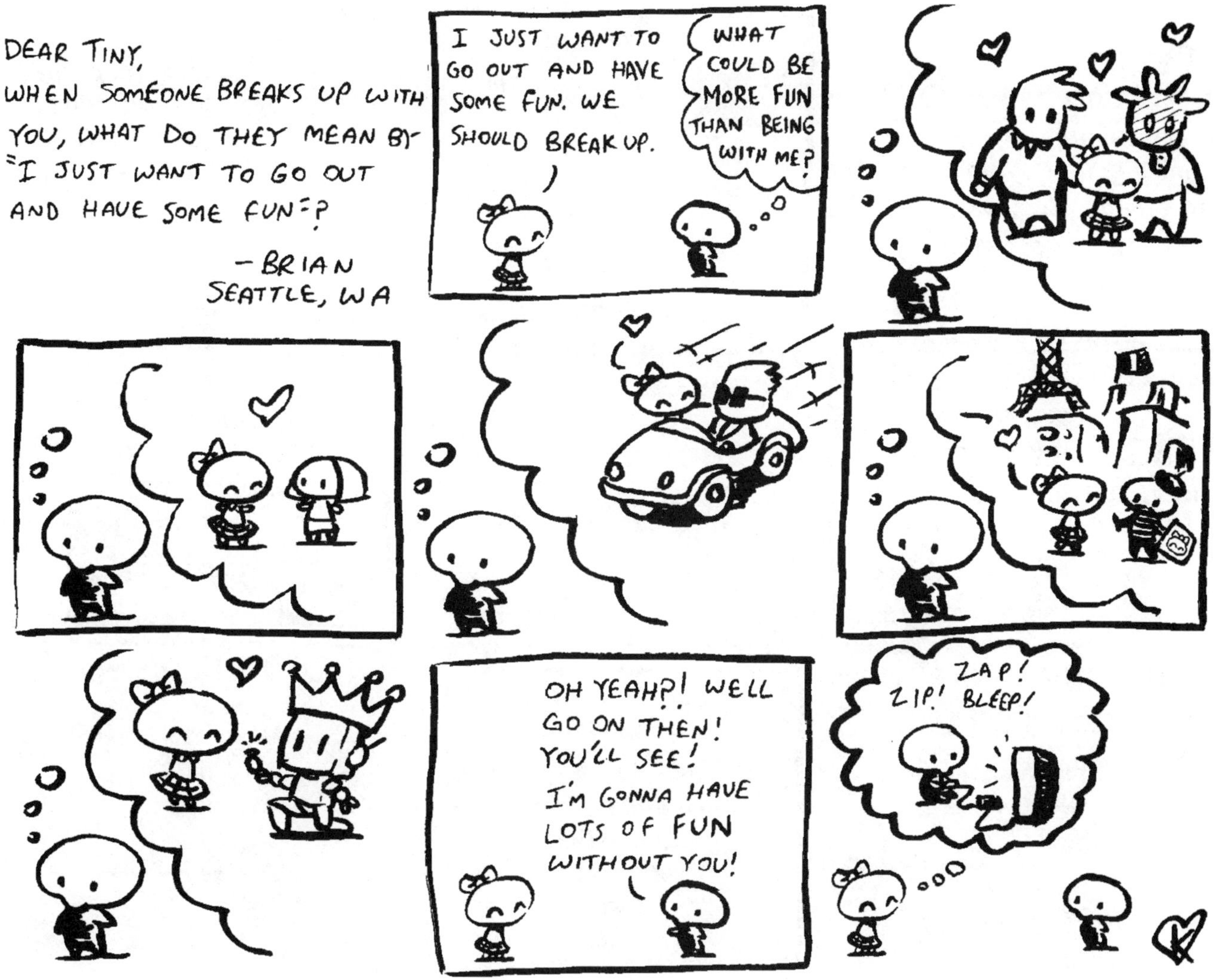
DEAR TINY,
WHEN SOMEONE BREAKS UP WITH YOU, WHAT DO THEY MEAN BY "I JUST WANT TO GO OUT AND HAVE SOME FUN"?
—BRIAN
SEATTLE, WA
I JUST WANT TO GO OUT AND HAVE SOME FUN. WE SHOULD BREAK UP.
WHAT COULD BE MORE FUN THAN BEING WITH ME?
OH YEAH?! WELL GO ON THEN! YOU'LL SEE! I'M GONNA HAVE LOTS OF FUN WITHOUT YOU!
ZIP! ZAP! BLEEP!

DEAR TINY,
HOW DO YOU HAVE A LOVING RELATIONSHIP WITH AN EVIL SUPERGENIUS WHO CAN DESTROY THE WORLD AT THE PUSH OF A BUTTON?
—LAURA SEATTLE, WA

HOW COULD YOU NOT BE IN LOVE WITH THESE KINDS OF GUYS?

THEY OWN COOL PADS...

YOU OWN THIS WHOLE ISLAND?

IT'S A TIME SHARE I HAVE WITH DR. NO AND SOME SOFTWARE GUYS.

COLLECT NEAT STUFF...

I LOVE YOUR VAN GOGH... WHAT'S THIS SHRIVELED THING BELOW IT?

HIS EAR.

THEY HAVE THE BEST VEHICLES...

SEE IF YOU CAN SPOT A SWIMMING POOL I CAN LAND THE "YACHT-COPTER" IN.

THEY KNOW THE MOST INTERESTING PEOPLE...

HE'S MY MAIN HENCHMAN... AND HE WRITES POETRY.

MOSTLY HAIKU.

THEY BUY THE MOST EXOTIC PETS...

"FIDO" IS THE ONLY SHARK-ADILE IN CAPTIVITY.

AND IF THESE THINGS AREN'T ENOUGH TO KEEP YOU IN LOVE WITH YOUR MADMAN, YOU CAN ALWAYS LEAVE HIM FOR A SUAVE SECRET AGENT...

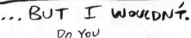

...BUT I WOULDN'T.

DO YOU MAKE GOLD STATUES OF ALL YOUR EX-GIRLFRIENDS?

ONLY THE ONES FIDO WON'T EAT.

DEAR TINY,
IS THERE REALLY ANY DIFFERENCE BETWEEN THE MESSED-UP DATING EXPERIENCES OF GAY MEN AND STRAIGHT WOMEN? MY BEST FRIEND IS STRAIGHT AND WE ALWAYS ONE UP EACH OTHER WITH OUR HORROR STORIES,
— CHANNING
S.L.C., UT

I DATED THIS GUY WHO NEVER BRUSHED HIS TEETH OR SHOWERED, AND WHO ONLY ATE GASSY FOODS.

I WENT OUT WITH AN ALCOHOLIC WHO KEPT STEALING FROM ME TO BUY MORE BOOZE.

I WENT OUT WITH A GUY WHO BROUGHT HIS WIFE AND KIDS WITH HIM ON OUR DATE.

I SAW A MOVIE WITH A GUY WHO MADE OUT WITH SOMEONE SITTING NEXT TO HIM THROUGH THE ENTIRE FILM.

I WENT HOME WITH THIS ONE GUY WHO POSTED PICTURES OF OUR ENCOUNTER ON THE INTERNET THE NEXT DAY.

HOW DO WE KEEP GETTING INTO THESE SITUATIONS?

HEY, YOU TWO WANT TO GO OUT TONIGHT? YES!!!

COOL, YOU'RE PAYING. SIGH... THAT'S HOW. THAT'S HOW WHAT?

127

DEAR TINY,
I AM VERY HAPPY IN MY
CURRENT RELATIONSHIP.
HOW LONG MAY I EXPECT
THIS TO LAST? IS THERE
A GRAPH?
    LOVE, ALEX
        BOULDER, CO

IF YOU LOOK AT THIS CHART,
CODEPENDENCY INCREASES
OVER TIME, BECOMING THE MAIN
REASON COUPLES LAST.

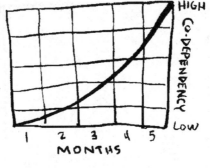

TINY,
HOW CAN GIRLS GET PAST
ALL THE IMAGES OF
BEAUTIFUL WOMEN THROWN
AT THEM EVERY DAY AND
STILL LOVE THEMSELVES FOR
WHO THEY ARE?   -SAMMIE

PSSST...
HEY KID.

DO YOU REALLY
WEAR THAT
IN PUBLIC?

YOU'D BETTER BUY
SOME CLOTHES FROM
THIS CENTURY HONEY.

AND WHAT'S
WITH THE
HAIR?

NO ONE WEARS
IT LIKE THAT
ANYMORE, SWEETIE.

YOU COULD ALSO
STAND TO LOSE
SOME WEIGHT
IN BACK, BABY.

SO NOW YOU KNOW
WHAT TO DO TO BE A
HAPPY GIRL, RIGHT?

YEAH,
THIS.

CLICK

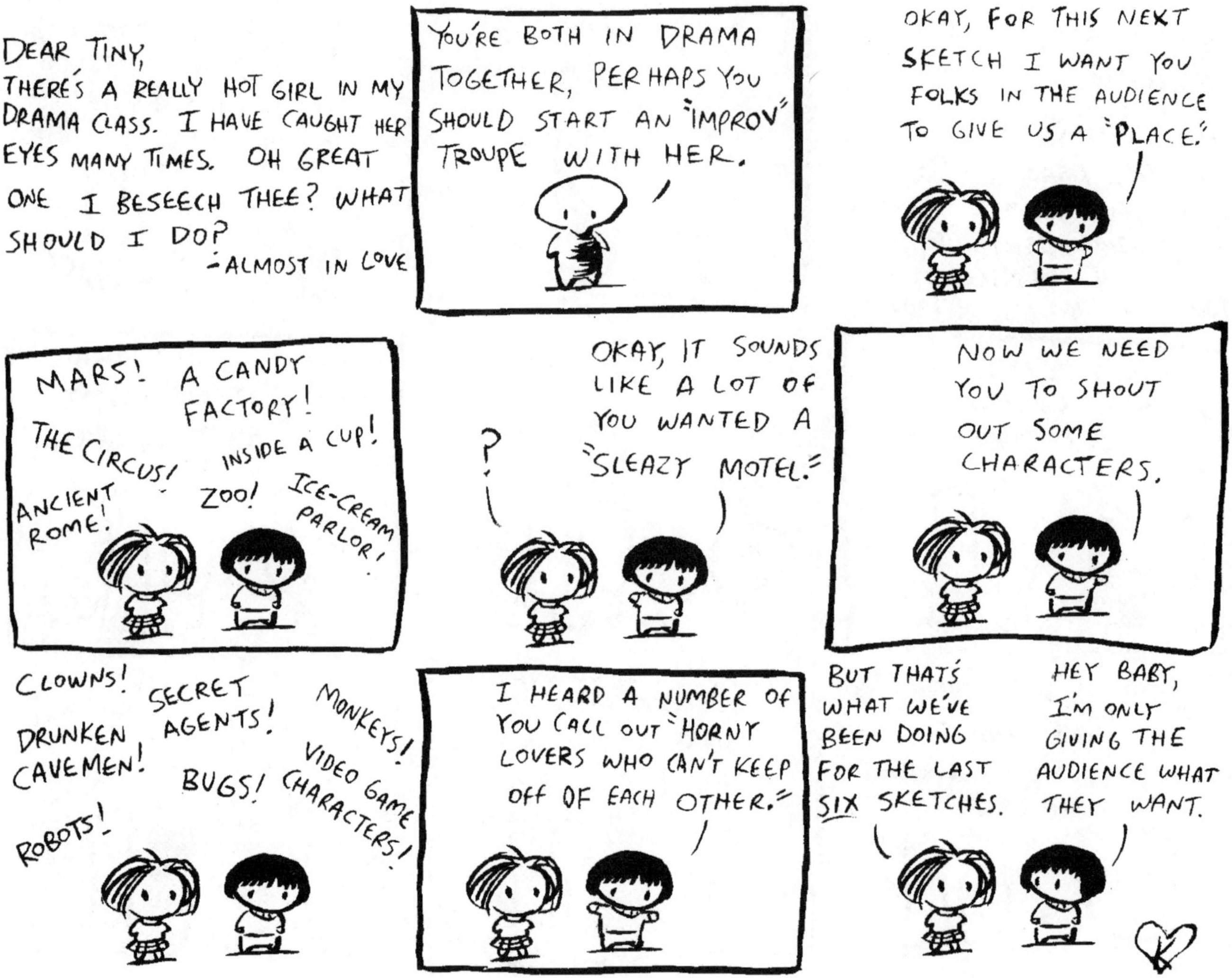

DEAR TINY,
THERE'S A REALLY HOT GIRL IN MY DRAMA CLASS. I HAVE CAUGHT HER EYES MANY TIMES. OH GREAT ONE I BESEECH THEE? WHAT SHOULD I DO?
-ALMOST IN LOVE
YOU'RE BOTH IN DRAMA TOGETHER, PERHAPS YOU SHOULD START AN "IMPROV" TROUPE WITH HER.
OKAY, FOR THIS NEXT SKETCH I WANT YOU FOLKS IN THE AUDIENCE TO GIVE US A "PLACE."
MARS!
A CANDY FACTORY!
THE CIRCUS!
INSIDE A CUP!
ANCIENT ROME!
ZOO!
ICE-CREAM PARLOR!
?
OKAY, IT SOUNDS LIKE A LOT OF YOU WANTED A "SLEAZY MOTEL."
NOW WE NEED YOU TO SHOUT OUT SOME CHARACTERS.
CLOWNS!
SECRET AGENTS!
MONKEYS!
DRUNKEN CAVEMEN!
VIDEO GAME CHARACTERS!
BUGS!
ROBOTS!
I HEARD A NUMBER OF YOU CALL OUT "HORNY LOVERS WHO CAN'T KEEP OFF OF EACH OTHER."
BUT THAT'S WHAT WE'VE BEEN DOING FOR THE LAST SIX SKETCHES.
HEY BABY, I'M ONLY GIVING THE AUDIENCE WHAT THEY WANT.

DEAR TINY,
EVERYDAY WE ATHLETES WAKE UP
AT 4:30 A.M. TO ROW INTO THE
ICE-COLD SNOHOMISH RIVER.
WITH SPRING APPROACHING, THE CREW
TEAM NEEDS MORE MEMBERS.
ANY IDEAS?
— EvCC CREW
EVERETT, WA

I CAN SEE WHY YOU
MIGHT HAVE PROBLEMS
RECRUITING NEW MEMBERS.

TRY SOME OF THESE
RECRUITING STRATEGIES
TO ATTRACT NEW TEAMMATES.

CONSIDER A LATER
PRACTICE TIME

ZZZZ! 12:36

FREE DOUGHNUTS AT
EACH DRILL

BREAKFAST
OF CHAMPIONS,
BABY!

REPLACE OARS WITH
AN OUTBOARD MOTOR

THIS IS SO
MUCH EASIER!
RRRRRRR!

MANDATORY PRACTICES AND
COMPETITIONS IN HAWAII

HEY, IT BEATS AN
ICE-COLD RIVER!

GET A DOMINATRIX
AS CREW CAPTAIN

STROKE FASTER,
MAGGOT!!!   YES
MA'AM!
CRACK!

REPACKAGE YOUR SPORT
AS "EXTREME"

STROKE!!!
STROKE!!!
WE'RE LOSING
ALTITUDE!
GRAND CANYON

DEAR TINY,
I LOVE MY GIRLFRIEND BUT THERE IS ANOTHER GIRL I'M INFATUATED WITH. WHEN I'M NOT WITH "GIRL #2" I FORGET ABOUT HER AND FOCUS ON MY HONEY. BUT WHEN I SEE HER I CAN'T HELP MYSELF. I CAN'T HAVE BOTH, SO WHAT CAN I DO?
—ANON.

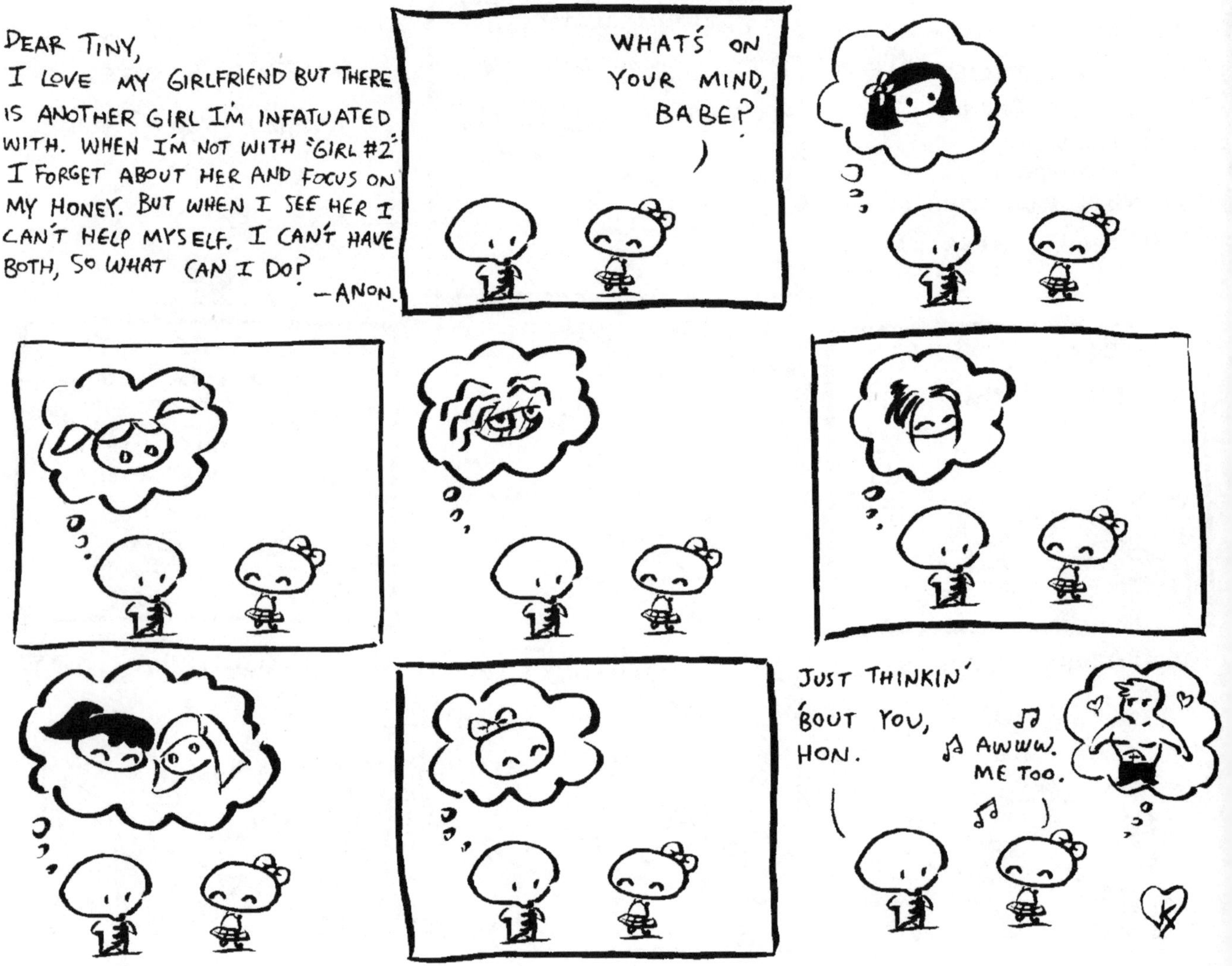
WHAT'S ON YOUR MIND, BABE?
JUST THINKIN' 'BOUT YOU, HON.
AWWW. ME TOO.

DEAR TINY,
WHAT WOULD BE THE BEST WAY FOR ME TO ASK OUT THE CUTE GIRL IN MY CLASS I HAVE NOTHING IN COMMON WITH?

— SCARED GUY
BOULDER, CO

PEOPLE WHO HAVE NOTHING IN COMMON OFTEN DATE EACH OTHER WITH NO PROBLEMS.

BUT IF YOU FEEL YOU NEED THAT INITIAL BOND, THEN HERE ARE A FEW SUGGESTIONS TO CONSIDER.

JOIN HER CLUBS

YOU WANT TO JOIN THE <u>WOMEN'S</u> VOLLEYBALL TEAM?

YOU BET!

SUPPORT HER CAUSES

I'M GLAD YOU VOLUNTEERED TO HELP OUT OUR PROTEST AGAINST THE MEAT INDUSTRY.

YEAH, THEIR PRICES ARE WAY TOO HIGH.

GET TO KNOW HER FRIENDS

REALLY?! SHE SAID SHE LIKES ME?!

NO. I WAS JUST KIDDING.

LEARN ABOUT HER BELIEFS

MY RELIGION TEACHES ME PHYSICAL AFFECTION IS A SIN.

WHAT IF YOU DO IT WITH NON-BELIEVERS?

OF COURSE, YOU MAY WANT TO AVOID TRYING TO HAVE TOO MUCH IN COMMON WITH HER.

ISN'T IT AMAZING HOW MUCH WE SHARE IN COMMON?

UH... SURE ... HELLO, POLICE?

DEAR TINY,
 I'VE BEEN WITH MY BOYFRIEND FOR SIX MONTHS. WE LIVE AND WORK TOGETHER AND I LOVE HIM WITH ALL MY HEART. BUT I HAVE AN IRRATIONAL FEAR THAT HE'S CHEATING ON ME, THOUGH HE'S NEVER DONE THAT IN HIS LIFE. HE'S A GREAT GUY. HOW CAN I GET OVER MY FEAR?
                        — FALLEN ANGEL

INFIDELITY IS A PRETTY COMMON INSECURITY FOR A LOT OF COUPLES.

BUT PERHAPS YOU SHOULD CONCERN YOURSELF WITH OTHER POSSIBLE SECRETS YOUR LOVER MAY BE CONCEALING FROM YOU.

WHAT YOU FOUND IN THE CLOSET LOOKS BAD, BUT I DON'T USE IT TO <u>PROBE</u> ANYTHING.

ALIEN?

HEY HON, COULD YOU PACK THIS BAG OF "FLOUR" IN YOUR SUITCASE? IT'S A SOUVENIR FOR GRANDMA.

SMUGGLER?

DID I SAY RITUAL SACRIFICE? I MEANT I'M GOIN' TO A MOVIE.

CULTIST?

DIDN'T YOU JUST LEAVE FOR WORK?

NOPE.

CLONE?

THIS IS MY LATE-NIGHT JOGGING SUIT. THE GRAPPLING HOOK IS JUST ORNAMENTAL.

SUPERHERO?

LOOK! ANOTHER COMIC ABOUT AN ARGUMENT WE HAD RECENTLY.

REALLY? WEIRD.

CARTOONIST?

DEAR TINY,

WHY DOES IT HURT WHEN I URINATE?

— BIG C
DALLAS, TX

YIKES! MAYBE YOU SHOULD GO SEE A DOCTOR!

OTHERWISE, TRY THESE PREVENTIVE MEASURES.

"NO MORE SULFURIC COCKTAILS!"

ESPECIALLY WITH HYDROCHLORIC CHASERS.

"REMOVE THAT THORN BUSH FROM YOUR TOILET."

"CEASE YOUR FAMOUS 'FLAME THROWER' TRICK."

OKAY, I DRANK A GALLON OF GASOLINE, NOW I NEED A MATCH!

"STOP USING STAPLES AS CHEAP EROTIC PIERCINGS."

THE REPORT IS STAPLED TO YOUR WHAT?!

"BROKEN GLASS BOTTLES ARE NOT A PORTABLE TOILET"

DID YOU FEEL THAT POTHOLE? ...UH OH...

"USE THE APPROPRIATE BATHROOM... ALWAYS."

OW! LADY! OW! HITTING ME WON'T MAKE IT GO ANY FASTER!

DEAR TINY,

I WAS IN A VERY INTENSE RELATIONSHIP WITH A GUY WHO WAS CHEATING ON ME. NOW THAT WE'RE APART I'M STILL HAUNTED BY MY FEELINGS FOR HIM. HOW CAN I GET OVER HIM? —KIMMY SF CA

THERE IS NO GETTING OVER. THERE IS ONLY GETTING ON.

DEAR TINY,
WHY DO MARRIED MEN FLIRT WITH SINGLE WOMEN?

—"J"
SAN FRANCISCO, CA

I ASKED THIS MARRIED GUY TO HELP EXPLAIN IT TO US.

HIYA, BEAUTIFUL.

I WANT TO START BY SAYING I NEVER FLIRT SERIOUSLY.

IT MAY BE HARD TO UNDERSTAND THE SUBTLE HUMOR OF MY ADVANCES, BUT IT'S JUST GOOD, CLEAN FUN.

I MEAN IT'S ABSURD THAT A MARRIED PERSON LIKE MYSELF WOULD EVER WANT ANOTHER RELATIONSHIP WITH A NEW LOVER.

I DON'T WANT TO ESCAPE FROM ONE PRISON JUST TO BREAK INTO ANOTHER. HAR-HAR!

I'M SURE THE IRONY IS LOST ON A LOT OF FOLKS OUT THERE.

SO TO YOU, FLIRTING IS A "JOKE"?

AND THE PUNCHLINE IS "TOO BAD I'M MARRIED". HA!

DON'T YOU THINK YOUR "JOKE" WILL JUST GET OLD AND ANNOYING TO PEOPLE?

WHAT, LIKE A COMIC ABOUT RELATIONSHIPS?

DEAR TINY,

MY GIRLFRIEND AND I ARE DOING OUR POST-DOCS IN LABS IN DIFFERENT COUNTRIES. WHAT CAN I DO TO KEEP OUR RELATIONSHIP STRONG?
— JASON
DALLAS, TX

ORBIT A SATELLITE AROUND HER

CLONE YOURSELF FOR HER

DOWNLOAD YOUR CONSCIOUSNESS ONTO HER COMPUTER

MAKE A TELEPORTER

INVENT A SHRINK RAY AND SEND YOURSELF TO HER.

BUILD AN ANTIGRAVITY ROCKET CAR

138

DEAR TINY,
IS UNDERWEAR AN
OPTION ON THE
FIRST DATE?
— J.D.

YES, IT IS AN OPTION.
HERE ARE SOME THINGS
YOU CAN WEAR INSTEAD.

BALOONS

IT'S LIKE WEARING
A PARTY WHERE
EVERYONE IS
INVITED.

SURGICAL MASK

WANNA
PLAY
DOCTOR?

PORTABLE T.V.

TOLD YA
I HAD
A 14 INCH
IN MY PANTS!

PUPPIES, BUNNIES, AND KITTIES

MEW...
SURE TO
LEAD TO
HEAVY
PETTING.

CHOCOLATE

NO, I DID
NOT HAVE
AN "ACCIDENT."

FISH BOWL

HEY...
THIS FEELS
NICE.

CEREAL BOX

THERE'S A
PRIZE IN
EVERY BOX,
BABY!

SUGAR
PUFFS

Dear Tiny,
I was recently offered a plane ticket to visit a guy I'm online buddies with across the country. What should I think of his offer?
— Mo
Knoxville, TN

Come visit me. I'll buy you a ticket.

I don't know if I should.

We really haven't met face to face yet.

We only know each other from emails, web cam shots, chats, and phone calls.

Why not?

It's a little much for me to go to a city I don't know, to meet someone I really haven't seen in person.

I still want to meet you, but someplace neutral and where I'd feel safe.

That sounds fair. Where should I get tickets to?

Hawaii!

DEAR TINY,
ARE GIRLS CRUEL ON PURPOSE, OR DO THEY JUST DO IT ACCIDENTALLY?
—SQUINTY

WHY WOULD ANYONE, BOY OR GIRL, BE CRUEL ON PURPOSE?

IT ALL MUST BE AN "ACCIDENT."

HON, WHY ARE THERE OTHER MEN'S UNDERWEAR IN MY DRAWER?

OOOPS. I MUST'VE PUT THEM THERE ON ACCIDENT.

HOW COULD YOU FORGET OUR WEDDING DAY?

SORRY. IT WAS AN ACCIDENT.

WHY DO YOU CRY OUT OTHER PEOPLE'S NAMES WHEN WE'RE TOGETHER?

JUST AN ACCIDENT.

YOU SECRETLY VIDEO TAPE US IN BED, AND SELL IT ONLINE? WHAT'S WRONG WITH YOU?!

IT WAS AN ACCIDENT, BABY.

IF YOU HAD NO INTENTION OF GETTING BACK TOGETHER, WHY DID YOU LEAD ME ON?

I DID IT BY ACCIDENT.

ACCIDENTS HAPPEN.

DEAREST SEPUKU,
I AM A NERVOUS DJ WHO WILL BE
SPINNING FOR MY FIRST TIME BEFORE
A THOUSAND OR MORE PEOPLE. I
DON'T WANT TO MESS UP BECAUSE OF
MY SHY CLUMSINESS. WHAT SHOULD
I DO TO OVERCOME MY FEAR OF
PERFORMING?
—SAMANTHA
AKA DJ GIRL

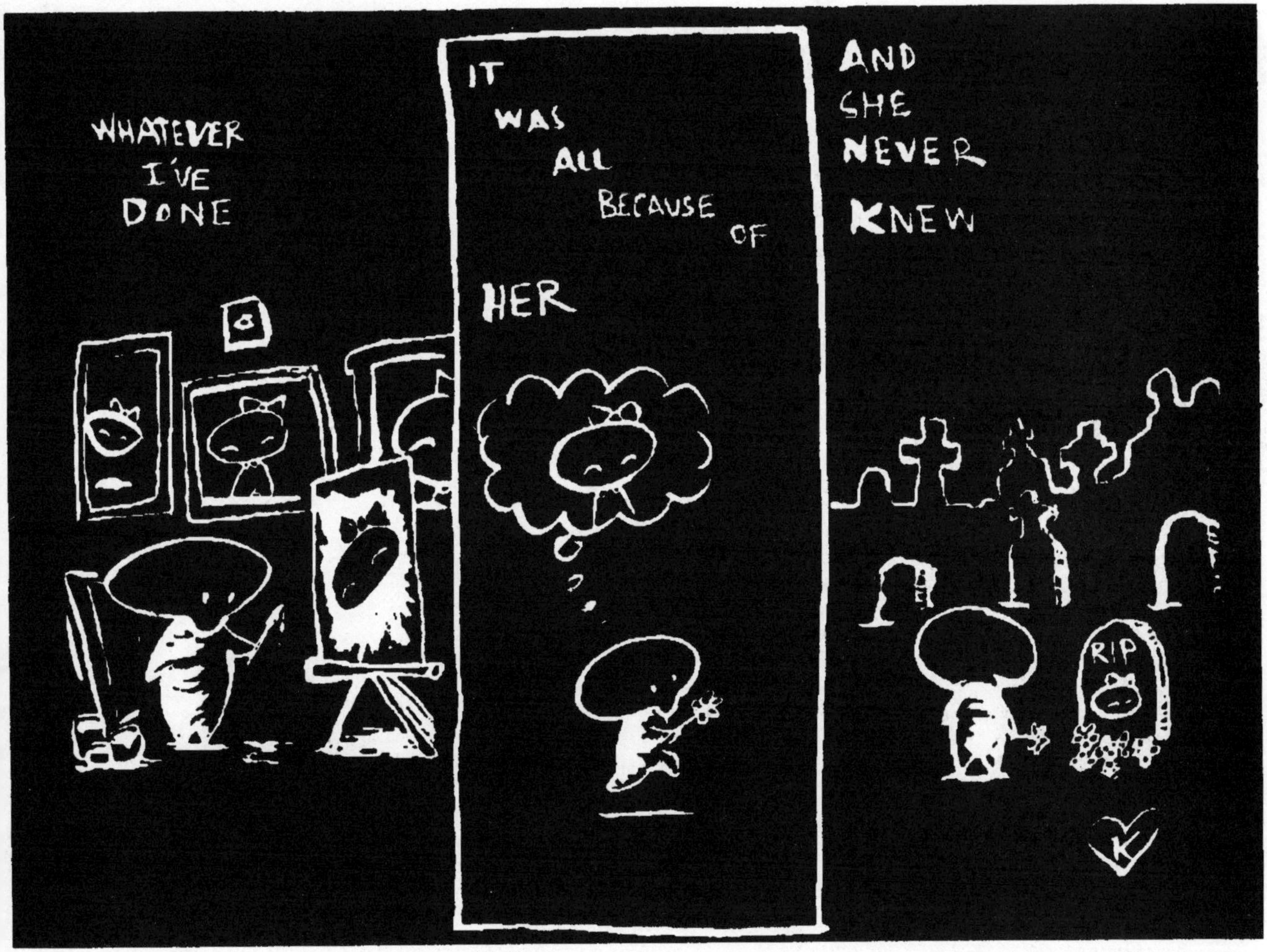
WHATEVER I'VE DONE
IT WAS ALL BECAUSE OF HER
AND SHE NEVER KNEW
RIP